25 TROPICAL HOUSES
in the Philippines

ELIZABETH V. REYES

introduction by PAULO ALCAZAREN

photographs by A. CHESTER ONG

PERIPLUS

Published by Periplus Editions, with
editorial offices at 130 Joo Seng Road
#06-01/03, Singapore 368357.

Text © 2005 Elizabeth V. Reyes
Photographs © 2005 A. Chester Ong

ISBN 0 7946 0315 7
Printed in Singapore

Distributed by:
Asia Pacific
Berkeley Books Pte Ltd, 130 Joo Seng
Road #06-01/03, Singapore 368357.
Tel: (65) 6280 1330; Fax: (65) 6280 6290
E-mail: inquiries@periplus.com.sg
http://www.periplus.com

*North America, Latin America
and Europe*
Tuttle Publishing, 364 Innovation Drive,
North Clarendon, Vermont 05759, USA.
Tel: (802) 773 8930; Fax: (802) 773 6993
E-mail: info@tuttlepublishing.com
http://www.tuttlepublishing.com

Japan
Tuttle Publishing, Yaekari Building, 3F,
5-4-12 Osaki, Shinagawa-ku, Tokyo
141-0032. Tel: (813) 5437 0171;
Fax: (813) 5437 0755
E-mail: tuttle-sales@gol.com

08 07 06 05
6 5 4 3 2 1

Page 1 Atrium house, Valle Verde, Pasig,
Metro Manila (page 82), architect
Eduardo Calma.

Page 2 Tengco townhouse, Forbes Park,
Makati City, Metro Manila (page 66),
designers Budji Layug and Royal Pineda.

Pages 4-5 Montinola pavilions, Forbes
Park, Makati City, Metro Manila (page 72),
architects Romeo Delfinado and
Andy Locsin.

Pages 6-7 Leviste lanai, Ayala Alabang,
Muntinlupa, Metro Manila (page 152),
architect Emmanuel Miñana; Escher
mansion, Ayala Alabang, Muntinlupa,
Metro Manila (page 136), architect Jorge
B. Yulo; Ngo house, Ayala Heights, Quezon
City, Metro Manila (page 56), architect
Joey Yupangco.

contents

the philippine house goes tropical modern

Modern residential architecture in tropical Asia generally and in the Philippines in particular is going through a fascinating phase of architectural evolution. Stylish new homes in Metropolitan Manila, the capital of the Philippines, and sultry waterside locations scattered around the archipelago's 7000 tropical islands, are providing plush living spaces for increasingly affluent Filipinos. These new houses have sparked a renaissance in residential architecture that is not only changing the Philippine suburban landscape but is also providing fodder for the imagination in international publications, pointing to a nascent design trend: "Tropical modern" is becoming the *new* modern.

Philippine "tropical modern" is characterized by residential designs that are distinctive in their use of mutable space, sensual local materials, and functional accommodation of hybrid East–West lifestyles. Echoing a pan-Asian trend and a larger trajectory for architectural development in tropical-belt countries, spaces in these homes show creative configurations of often-minimal spaces. Filipino architects and designers are also offering fresh approaches in the use of materials and architectural elements that cater to both the changing cosmopolitan tastes of an ever more discerning Filipino élite and the aspirations of a progressive, budget-conscious middle class. Tropical modern design is affordably "cool."

"Cool" means more than fashionable façades and hip interiors. It includes environmental friendliness. In their search for this, Filipino architects are constantly experimenting with new materials and techniques or rediscovering almost-forgotten materials and traditional arts and crafts expertise. Cross-ventilation, sun screens, wide eaves, raised floors, and sensitive solar orientation—devices long used in local vernacular architecture, perhaps unknowingly—are now given a contemporary twist with the use of steel instead of bamboo, concrete and fiberboard instead of woven mats, glass and plastics instead of *capiz* shells. These older vernacular materials are not being discarded but are instead being processed in new ways with lamination, machine weaving, heat tempering and shaping to produce attractive building materials. Passive cooling, solar power, recycled gray water, and ventilated roofs are being rationally employed in house designs. Tropical modern is not only architecturally "modern" and affordably "cool," it is also "green."

Right "Bellavista," the modernist house of Eirvin and Josephine Knox (page 44), casts long afternoon shadows and a trajectory for design development. Architect Ed Calma offers creative configurations of minimalist spaces, using cubist elements that cater to the changing cosmopolitan tastes of a discerning Filipino élite.

Above The glamorous residence
of Gunn and Cris Roque (page 26)
is characterized by fluid lines and
Art Deco notions, plus the unifying
element of wide *narra* stairs cascading like rice terraces down
through the house. Designer Budji
Layug demonstrates here his
"Tropical Modern" philosophy.

Cultural color is another big factor in the designs of these tropical modern homes. The interiors and exteriors address, both spatially and socially, the lifestyles that Filipinos (as well as many other Asians elsewhere), have grown to know and enjoy. Modern Filipinos adopt Western life, work, and leisure styles to fit cultural norms and social nuances. The demands of the extended family, the need to frequently entertain during the Philippines' numerous festive occasions, the projection of social standing and roles in the community, and the concept of *hiyá* (face) are intertwined with Western or modern practicalities such as the acceptance of home/office setups, a reduced dependence on domestic help, and the advent of two-career households, multiple-vehicle garages, and modern communications technology. Tropical modern merges cyberspace with traditional cultural space, at the same time retaining the best of both.

The single most important factor, however, that differentiates one tropical modern Philippine home from another relates to site—and the Filipino architects' response to this. Whether the site is a sprawling suburban lot, a small urban core, or an idyllic resort locale well away from Metropolitan Manila with a romantic name like Punta Fuego or Calatagan, the final design of a house is influenced by the site: its size, the limitations imposed by its shape and topography, its location in relation to neighboring sites, its solar and wind orientation, its exposure to seasonal rains, the ease of its access, its potential for views, and its overall visual impact.

Regardless of variations in site, the thrust of this new architectural movement is largely expressed in the styles and themes that consistently recur in Philippine interior design. In contrast to the traditional modernist absence of edge treatments, a leitmotif common to many of the houses shown in this book, notably those designed by Ramon Antonio, Francisco Mañosa, and Andy Locsin, is the use of stained wood frames for openings, thresholds, windows, and cabinetwork. Mostly made of Philippine hardwoods such as *narra*, *molave*, and *tanguile*, these frames provide a welcome contrast to classic modernist white or light-colored interiors. Another constant is the use of bright colors as accents or overall treatments in large areas (in the manner of modernist Mexican architect Luis Barragan) without diluting the essence and lines of the architectural design. Houses designed by Milo Vasquez, Joey Yupangco, Benji Reyes, and Marta Pedrosa exhibit this chromatic tendency, albeit in different color choices and combinations—leaning toward warmer but still colorful tones.

Within these houses and their framed spaces, the renaissance that has occurred in Philippine furniture design is showcased. A new generation of multitalented Filipino furniture and industrial designers, as well as designer-architects, is producing cutting-edge products that rework familiar, sometimes modernist, silhouettes in traditional materials such as rattan, bamboo, fiber, and wood. Notable among the trendsetters featured in this book are Budji Layug, one of the founders of designer group Movement 8, and Benji Reyes, known for his skill with large wooden pieces and the detail of his joinery. Groups like Movement 8 have banded together to expose this new wave to a global market, and with so much success that Western publications now regularly feature their pieces. These smaller-scaled products of Filipino creativity and their acceptance is a prelude to the entry of Philippine tropical modernism into Western and the wider global design discourse.

Right Fernando and Catherine Zobel's elegant rest house in Calatagan, Batangas (page 120), resembles a Japanese temple in a field. The house embodies the much-vaunted Asian Modern look produced by the Leandro V. Locsin firm: a sleek vernacular roofline, a rectilinear living space, and serene pavilions formed by planes of stone, glass, and water.

The innovative adaptation of materials as well as modern furniture and fixture design is carried through to the décor, embellishments, bathroom fixtures, water features, and landscape treatments in a home. This reflects a Filipino (and Asian) heritage of building that has always been sensitive to and respectful of nature. Traditional *koi* ponds, cascades, reflecting pools, and fountains are recast in modern shapes and used to add texture, movement, and sound, to complement volumes and mirror façades, or simply to provide kinetic relief. Nature and the landscape are brought into interior spaces via water play in toilets and baths, where many innovative permutations of washbasins in stone, glass, or metal, some oversized, some in sculptural masses or assemblages, are a radical departure from traditional bathroom fittings. Eduardo Calma, Royal Pineda, and Jorge Yulo, among the designers featured in this book, have produced elegant, sometimes quirkily humorous examples of these.

Ethnic décor in fabric, metal, and wood are reworked in (again) modern frames or inserted as accents or layers in furniture, partition panels, room dividers, or screens. Francisco Mañosa, Noel Saratan, and Ramon Antonio have a talent for mixing and matching, putting together a *bricolage* that completes the tropical modern *mise en scène*.

Tropical modern does not eschew all things Western and, in fact, provides settings that embrace Western furniture, architectural elements, or décor. The interiors of contemporary Philippine houses are often accented with selected Western furnishing and "branded" set pieces by the likes of Michael Graves or Philippe Starck. It is the heterotopic nature of modern Filipino design that actually provides a more layered reading and enjoyment of the spaces provided—compared to singular themes in Western interiors. The overall look and mood, despite these imports, is unmistakably tropical modern, pointing to another distinctive feature of Philippine houses: an eclectic design flexibility that allows references to Western art and objects without losing local stylistic identity.

As with design in most post-colonial countries, this identity has been over half a century in the making. For 300 years, the Philippines was under Spanish rule, followed by close to another fifty under the Americans. House design during this time was largely in the vernacular tradition, save for the residences of aristocrats in the cities. The Spanish house was adapted as the *bahay na bato* (literally "house of stone," but in reality stone on the ground floor and timber above), a vernacular house with Western-influenced architectural dress made more permeable to cooling winds and protected from the sun and rain. With the Americans came reinforced concrete and multistory apartments, mainly constructed in the Art Deco style, and bungalows in a gamut of revivalist styles, among them Italianate, Swiss Chalet, and Mission. A few schooled local architects, like Juan Arellano and Juan Nakpil, picked up where the Americans left off and carried residential design into the new urban morphological form of the suburb and residential subdivision or gated community.

As the 1950s brought independence to many Asian countries, each sought to strengthen its national identity in various ways, including through architecture. Modern architecture had, however, already established a firm foothold through the influence of local architects trained abroad. Frank Lloyd Wright, Le Corbusier, and the Bauhaus School influenced postwar architects to adopt flat roofs, bands of windows, and piloti (stilts) for buildings. Residential architecture in the Philippines took the form of California ranch homes and

Japanese and Hawaiian themed bungalows. It was only in the 1960s, when nationalism reared its head, that architects such as the Mañosa brothers, Felipe Mendoza, and Otilio Arellano sought to rediscover both their cultural roots and the tenets of vernacular design. These architects mined traditional roof shapes and embellishment patterns, mainly from the southern islands of the Philippines with strong Islamic influences.

Styles then swung from Spanish colonial housing models to American- and European-influenced geometric blocks predating the post-modern style. Synthetic adobe formed dark, heavy lower floors of suburban houses. Wide overhangs and eaves were used in predominantly horizontal compositions that mimicked Prairie-style architecture, with ornate Philippine mahogany and arcaded partitions. Many designers had difficulty reconciling tradition with modernity. Nonetheless, this era produced notable work by Andy Locsin and Gabriel Formoso, William Coscolluela and Ben Bautista, amongst others. In the 1990s, houses became brighter, lighter, and more practical in terms of energy use and function. Architectural education also improved, with students now more exposed to trends in the West, to growing research in Philippine architectural history, and to regional variations.

These conditions as well as the emergence of a new generation of Filipino designers have produced modern tropical residential architecture probably in the widest range of housing types to be found anywhere in Asia, among them urban bungalows, modern atria and courtyard houses, pavilion houses, townhouses, and minimalist tropical structures.

Within established central city districts or their immediate periphery in the Philippines can be found urban bungalows that cleverly generate space from lots limited to between 300 and 500 square meters because of high real estate values. Most of the ground floor of these bungalows is taken up by two-car garages, servants' quarters, and laundry areas, reducing the living areas at this level. Nevertheless, a feeling of spaciousness is achieved by generous glazing on two or more sides, bringing in light and melding the outside space with the indoors. This is seen in the Pasola-Gonzalez house by Budji Layug (page 162) and is used to great effect in the Glass residence by Ramon Antonio (page 204).

More usable space in this tropical typology is achieved by stacking space in mezzanines and lofts. In the classic modernist manner, the lack of outdoor space and gardens is compensated by locating them up high, on decks. With improved construction and waterproofing technology, these elevated terraces and gardens replace what would normally be pitched roofs. The Luz Studio home by Eduardo Calma (page 146) and the Ngo house by Joey Yupangco (page 56) are good examples of this strategy.

In older suburban districts as well as in the more exclusive residential gated enclaves, larger plots spawn modern courtyard configurations derived from Asian vernacular precedents, or large atrium-centered and inward-looking spaces that emulate palatial architecture. The courtyards in these houses serve as settings for ground-floor entertainment or as the focus of upper-floor viewing. Outdoor spaces are defined by variations in the way houses are massed into L, C, or U shapes. Their borders are delineated by vegetation or perimeter fencing, oftentimes taking advantage of neighboring landscapes to extend the space visually beyond the boundaries of the property. This strategy has been employed to perfection in the Martinez-Miranda house designed by Anna Maria Sy and Jason Chai (page 198).

Left The modernist white abode of designers Tes Pasola and Tony Gonzales (page 162) was shaped by their Movement 8 leader Budji Layug. He wrapped the functions of the house in a transparent "skin" of glass, affording it extra dimension, creative openness, and stimulation for artists. The *sala* is a gallery for art by Impy Pilapil (marble sculpture), Ann Pamintuan (wire seat), Ingo Maure (paper chandelier), and Milo Naval (abaca-weave coffee table). The abstract painting is by Tony Gonzales.

Full courtyards have also come back into vogue. A number of these new houses, like the Dee residence by Conrad Onglao (page 18), are so expansive that their atria form just one part of a series of spaces. Such volumetric expressions have antecedents in communal vernacular houses in Southeast Asia. Since these dwellings usually house more than one family, it is possible to think of them as a modern revival, fulfilling the need to define and confirm kinship by sharing space.

An abundance of space provides opportunities for large landscaped gardens to enhance the modern tropical dwellings set within them as well as appropriate settings for freestanding pavilions. The Montinola house designed by Romeo Delfinado and Andy Locsin (page 72) showcases such pavilions, here used for entertaining, dining, or simply reading. The pavilions are linked to the main house by covered walkways with large overhangs, producing, in effect, one continuous verandah.

The designs of these resort-like pavilion homes are undoubtedly influenced by the numerous resorts that have sprung up in Southeast Asia, the now almost generic Amans and Hyatts in Bali, Bangkok, and even Borobodur, that have become favorite destinations for both local and foreign holiday-makers. Images of pampered hospitality and sun-dappled splendor have become stock features of design magazines and coffee-table books worldwide. Pavilion homes carry the same amenities as their larger cousins—spas, pools, sunning decks, and outdoor baths—but on a smaller scale. The resort-style Verandah house by Milo Vazquez (page 104) and the Zobel hacienda by Ed Ledesma and Andy Locsin (page 120) project an ambience well suited to such publications.

Another design direction under the rubric of tropical modern—minimalist modernism, albeit a seemingly revivalist strain—is also gaining ground. Stark, all-white modernist boxes, design allusions to Mies van der Rohe, Le Corbusier, and Richard Meier, are being introduced in the suburbs and outskirts of tropical Metropolitan Manila, signaling an alternative path taken by a growing number of Asian clients whose lifestyles are defined by "less is more" and the projection of restrained, moneyed elegance. Minimalist interiors, a limited number of materials (usually only glass, stone, and metal), and expanses of glass define these houses. The seacoast setting of the Knox house by Eduardo Calma (page 44) maximizes its minimalist modern mien.

The materials, embellishments, and furniture used in these minimalist homes come from the same palette, leading one to believe that further evolution will take place as experimentation with this style continues. Already adaptations can be seen in response to the problem of preventing white surfaces from staining, minimizing the glare from white surfaces, selecting garden designs that complement rather than conflict with modern geometries, and finding solutions to the same problems with flat roofs that beset the first introduction of modernist styles in the 1960s. This experimentation has also seen adaptations from architectural solutions used in other tropical regions, including hot dry desert climates, and using simplified forms, as evident in the Pedrosa courtyard house (page 98). As the examples of these experiments multiply, so too will post-occupancy evaluations that will provide feedback to the designers on the possible approaches to this trajectory's functional and aesthetic evolution. This will eventually lead to greater public acceptance.

dee residence

"Think of an architect as a medium, not a signature. My designs are driven by a sense of scale and proportion, not style. We do what the client is comfortable living with. We interpret, not impose. We are flexible and versatile depending on a client's interaction and trust." CONRAD ONGLAO

Beng & Rikki Dee

CORINTHIAN GARDENS,
QUEZON CITY, METRO MANILA

ARCHITECT CONRAD ONGLAO
CT ONGLAO ARCHITECTS

Left The grandeur of the house derives from the use of white marble combined with solid black frames, as in these Mondrian-influenced sliding doors—repro art using different textured glass—leading to the dining area.

Above A glass bridge across the atrium—the symmetrical center of the interior architecture—forms a dramatic passageway, connecting the two side masses.

In recent years, new residential projects have been forced by lack of space to move from the traditional élite haven of Makati City to the upcoming entrepreneurs' communities of Ortigas and Quezon City. Well-traveled restaurateurs Beng and Rikki Dee had seen the homes of fellow entrepreneurs in Makati, and decided to build their house in the same genre. They eagerly gave free rein to architect Conrad Onglao to design a modernist structure in Quezon City, which combined comfort with dramatic impact. The result is a bold complex of concrete, glass, and marble cubist boxes with a classical configuration but on a scale that makes the house ideal for entertaining.

Their big white house, on a prime 1500-square meter corner lot, comprises a classical central mass flanked by two similar but smaller masses. A stylized white picket fence provides a fanciful domestic reference to the sculptural but neutral geometry of the architecture. Horizontal sunshades and concrete balconies add a modern touch.

Above right A bold black cantilevered staircase, without railings, sprouts from the white wall. The solid plank steps in a matte black finish ascend to the bedrooms on the upper floor.

Below right The restaurateur couple entertain in this formal dining room replete with multiple framed mirrors, a sleek ten-seater dining set, and a modernist chandelier overhead.

Above A clear view runs through the white marble interior—under the glass bridgeway—from the front entry at right to the formal sitting room at left.

Right The double-height atrium makes a perfect setting for the classic baby grand and a minimalist painting by Lao Lian Ben. The repetitive vertical lines in the wall divider replay the cubist theme.

From the front entrance, the house soars to a double-height atrium-foyer, a perfect setting for a baby grand. A dramatic glass-lined bridgeway crosses the foyer overhead, connecting the two side masses. Straight ahead, a clear view runs through the glass-walled mansion to a strip lawn on the north, revealing a separate Japanese-themed pavilion that appears to float on a long lap pool.

The atrium is the symmetrical center of the interior architecture. To one side, the formal *sala* is furnished along classic modernist lines (by the house-proud owners themselves) with the far wall forming a wide picture window framing the garden. To the right, within the opposite mass, a staircase made of matte black planks, cantilevered from a white wall, ascends to the upper floor. From there, a cluster of bedrooms connects with the large master suite via the glass-bottomed bridgeway over the central foyer.

The architect uses contemporary materials—concrete, glass, and stone—in a bold but neutral palette, while manipulating their scale, proportion, and symmetry. Part of the grandeur of the house derives from the use of white marble combined with solid black frames, which define

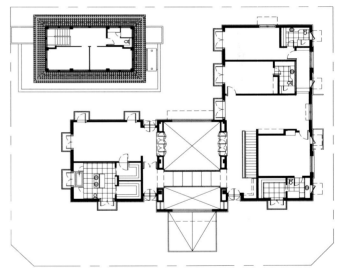

Above By night the artfully lit translucent glass bridgeway plays a different tune as it crosses toward the master suite. The vibrant painting at the end of the passage is by Impy Pilapil.

Above right Second floor plan.

Left The patio leads to a garden landscaped by Ponce Veridiano. The white picket fence provides a domestic reference for the neutral geometry of the architecture, while horizontal sunshades add a modern touch.

Below The classic modern mansion by night. Three modules—a central mass flanked by two similar but smaller masses—are combined on an impressive scale to make the big white house an ideal setting for entertaining.

Above right The informal side of the Dee lifestyle is reserved for the pavilion "floating" behind the main house. This Japanese-style gazebo serves as a lounge for the lap pool which is wrapped around it, as a casual luncheon hall, and as a home spa.

Below right Front elevation of the Dee residence.

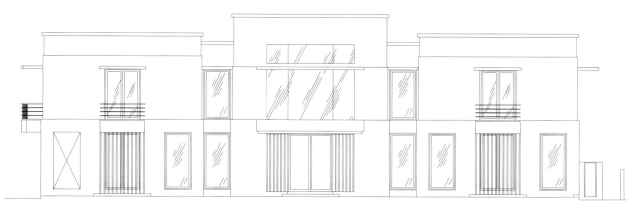

the expansive spaces. Onglao has made a design signature of the vertical scale of passages in his projects: all sliding doors stretch from floor to ceiling, allowing the visual space to flow unencumbered. Another hallmark is his use of cubist themes: the repetitive vertical lines on the outer fence reappear inside, in slatted wall dividers. The multi-mirrored dining room beyond the stairs is framed by two tall black sliding door panels, designed after Piet Mondrian paintings, but here "colored" with different textured glass.

The informal side of the Dee lifestyle takes places in a separate entertainment pavilion "floating" behind, and to one side, of the main house. This Japanese-style glass and iron gazebo, with its quirky hipped bamboo roof, acts as a lounge for the pool wrapped around it as well as a casual dining hall or games room for the whole family. Upstairs, there is a private spa for home massages. The gazebo is thus a perfect venue for the Dee family's lifestyle of food, fitness and well-being.

roque residence

"Every project is unique. But to design a home to suit a property's given characteristics, one that at the same time evokes sensual delight, is a challenge. For this site, which had great natural potential, our objective was to design a house in harmony with the surroundings." BUDJI LAYUG

Deep in Quezon City, tucked in the shadows of massive government buildings, is a long, 3000-square meter property on which is built a thriving garment business and a delightful home. Workaholic owners Gunn and Cris Roque were expanding their fashion enterprise and their family when they decided to build their home on an undeveloped back lot, close to yet removed from their workaday world.

The couple wanted a home that would showcase what they considered the best available in modern Asian design: furniture created by popular designer Budji Layug and new works by members of Movement 8, Layug's design colleagues. The Roque residence was the first house that Layug had built from the ground up after completing the award-winning pueblo-style Zulueta home on the slopes

Gunn & Cris Roque

BATASAN HILLS, QUEZON CITY, METRO MANILA

DESIGNERS BUDJI LAYUG & ROYAL PINEDA
BUDJI LAYUG+ROYAL PINEDA DESIGN ARCHITECTS

Above Sinuous lines and organic spaces flow through this remarkable split-level residence. The house straddles the natural mound fronting the entrance, while a crescent-shaped swimming pool wraps around the curved *sala* pavilion.

Below The family den-cum-television room in the second curved pavilion overlooks a view of the main curved *sala* pavilion "afloat" the crescent-shaped swimming pool, a recent addition by architect Royal Pineda. In the foreground is a modern Yin–Yang chair by Kenneth Cobonpue.

Bottom The informal *lanai* on the lowest level is furnished in Budji Layug and Royal Pineda's much-vaunted "Tropical Modern" style. The sofa set with matching ottoman is designed by Evolve, the solid wood coffee table by Claude Tayag, the abaca woven rug by Soumak, and the paper art pieces by Mind-masters.

Right The massive curved picture window in the grand *sala* allows a sweeping view of the crescent-shaped pool and the garden beyond. All interiors were custom designed and accessorized by Budji Layug, while the garden was landscaped by Ponce Veridiano.

Deep in Quezon City, tucked in the shadows of massive government buildings, is a long, 3000-square meter property on which is built a thriving garment business and a delightful home. Workaholic owners Gunn and Cris Roque were expanding their fashion enterprise and their family when they decided to build their home on an undeveloped back lot, close to yet removed from their workaday world.

The couple wanted a home that would showcase what they considered the best available in modern Asian design: furniture created by popular designer Budji Layug and new works by members of Movement 8, Layug's design colleagues. The Roque residence was the first house that Layug had built from the ground up after completing the award-winning pueblo-style Zulueta home on the slopes

of Tagaytay in 1983. The house took two years to conceptualize and complete—down to the last piece of art.

Making the most of the limitations imposed by the site, and working within a concept which he calls "organic-modern," Layug designed a curvilinear 750-square meter split-level house on the naturally rocky property. At the entrance is a large rock mound, from which the house flows in an L shape. The front elevation is a multilayered grouping of clean, dark-colored modernist roofs over a sand-colored resort-like structure. At both ends, the central volume flares outward to curved "pavilions" with expansive picture glass windows. Bordering the main living room pavilion are rounded Art Deco corners—features that give the house its retro "organic" flavor. At the back of the

Right The rounded form of the *sala* pavilion, here reflected in the new swimming pool, exudes an organic and Art Deco air. On the right is the entrance to the kitchen and the peripheral wall with a sleek new terrace landscape.

Above left Every angle of the dominant spiraling central staircase makes a graphic statement. Here, the wide steps lead from the dining area to the *lanai* on the ground floor.

Below Ground floor plan.

Above right This section of the staircase leads from the bedrooms on the second level down past a gallery corner displaying a stone and marble sculpture by Impy Pilapil.

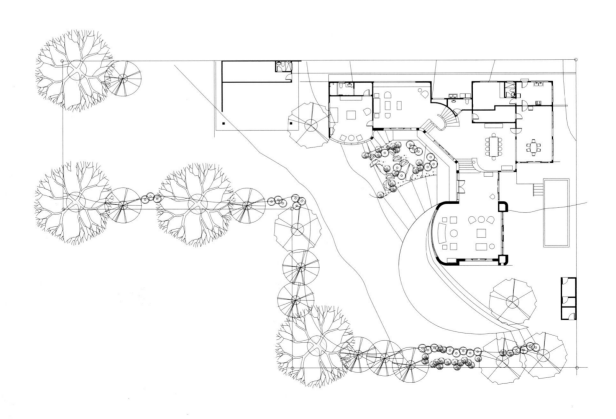

Above Inspired by rice terraces, the luxurious staircase curves down gracefully to the dining mezzanine, to greet a pivotal and pregnant white column on a rounded base.

Right The formal dining area features a magnificent red *narra* wood floor, a solid *narra* wood table from Claude Tayag, and a gilded abstract mural by artist Gus Albor.

Left The curved edge of the swimming pool is visible from the deck outside the master suite. The pool is surrounded by manicured lawns and well-tended gardens.

Below left The second floor plan of the Roque residence shows the house pushed back against two adjacent sides of the lot.

Above right The crescent-shaped swimming pool is a picturesque *tour de force* by architect Royal Pineda. The custom-made blue-green tiling was manufactured by Manila contractor FNSP.

Below right Pineda's landscaping at the rear of the house opened up the kitchen to a new sandstone tiled terrace. A modular two-level water feature flows gently into the children's wading pool below. Fine bamboo softens the high perimeter wall.

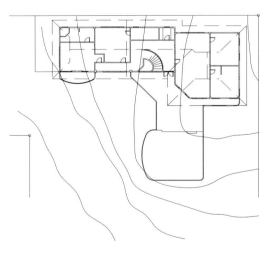

The grand "terraces" flow through the dining area—a raised platform of gleaming *narra* wood—then swirl by a gently rounded Art Deco column atop a curving base, before turning back sharply and flowing down toward a lower den-cum-television room located in the second curved pavilion. Standing near the front entry, the white column on the mezzanine is the axis of the L-shaped house. From its base the space sprawls outward to the main *sala* pavilion with its massive curved picture glass window. There the living setting is a showcase for the tropical modern furnishings by the designers of Movement 8.

The outside of the Roque residence was recently altered and modernized along the same organic theme by Layug's business partner, architect Royal Pineda. He reconfigured the landscape from the entrance to the rear garden, removing the jungly waterfall, improving access to the kitchen, and adding a spacious tiled terrace at the back. He also designed a stunning crescent-shaped swimming pool with blue-green tiles which echoes the shape of the curved glass window in the living room pavilion, and which descends to the deep end via three layers of curved steps.

Pineda explains the new landscape: "The swimming pool fronting the house is the first thing that people notice. Following the curvilinear lines of the house, it was made into a crescent shape and wrapped close to the main *sala* pavilion so that the house could be reflected in its waters. At the entrance to the property, the existing rock formation with a new water fountain is used as a natural point of interest and as a contrast to the new crescent pool." By night, glowing glass pavilions appear to "float" upon the reflective waters of the pool.

Two complementary styles are now evident in the home: Layug's original interior with its terraced stairway flowing among stunning settings, and Pineda's modern crescent pool and terrace that mixes disciplined modernism with a fresh use of space. Together, they form a picturesque home—the inner scheme in harmony with the landscape.

sy house

"Light is an element we tend to play with in our projects. Natural light filtering through the house, by way of light voids or punctures, relieves dependency upon artificial lighting during the day. Illumination enhances spatial experience, imbuing spaces with calmness, repose, and inner peace." JOEY YUPANGCO

Ricky & Veronica Sy

DASMARIÑAS VILLAGE, MAKATI CITY, METRO MANILA

ARCHITECT JOEY YUPANGCO, JY+A

Well-known modernist Joey Yupangco describes this home in Makati City as "a house like the face of Janus" because it has two very different faces, two orientations. "This time the rear became the front." The original family home was a spacious Filipino-Spanish 1980s bungalow complete with red shingles on the roof and wrought iron over the windows. The challenge for designer Yupangco was to create a contiguous unit *within* the big old house where a young professional couple could enjoy a lifestyle reflecting their tastes and interests. His design resulted in a radically different modernist unit inserted within the existing framework, sharing the same roof as the original house, but outfitted in a completely different style. The front elevation remains the original family home, but the rear façade reflects the new generation's design interests: functional minimalism,

Japanese sensibility, linearity, contemporary materials (aluminum, concrete, and frosted glass), and natural light.

From the front of the house, the fusion is subtle. A massive plinth in naked concrete is set under the wide roof fascia. The new space then emerges within the old, first glimpsed through the front door as a transformation in space and materials. The space has been deconstructed and rebuilt as a glass-lined, minimalist apartment. What was low-slung and cozy in the 1980s has been reborn long and tall in soaring vertical lines, bathed with light from above, floored with expanses of polished concrete and white stone, and walled with glass paneling from end to end.

The linear interior derives its theme from modern Japanese design, visible in the sliding panels and doors, the aluminum framing on glass, and the "folded walls and ceilings" (smacking of origami) on the upper level. At the center of the double-height atrium, a lofty skylight contains a "suspended sculpture box"—the designer's centerpiece and the main point of visual interest in the duplex—that refracts light falling into the space.

Home owners Ricky and Veronica Sy enjoy an informal lifestyle, hanging around the open kitchen together or with friends, dining on an extra-long worktable, and listening to music in the audiovisual den. Yupangco deliberately

Left In the sleek living/dining/work area under the mezzanine, industrial glass walls meet concrete floors in a stunning display of functional minimalism. At right is a full wall of storage under translucent slide-away panels. A worktable is cantilevered to the central post.

Right At the back of the long apartment, light shines strongly through translucent glass curtain walls. Bold, colorful standing lamps provide the only ornamentation in the sparse space.

Right The sculptural boxes suspended high up in the atrium are Yupangco's modernist "lamps"— architectural elements designed to both accent the giant skylight and to filter the light pouring into the interior.

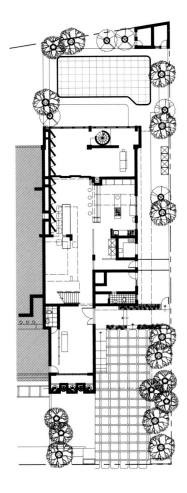

Far left "Brutalist" or raw concrete walls—formed in place—and large windows shielded by micro-mesh shades and trees make for an unusual treatment in the master bathroom. The porcelain sinks and the innovative wooden bathtub are by Agape.

Left The ground floor plan shows the linearity of the site and house.

Below The lounging area at the rear is where the owners entertain close friends. The spiral staircase which climbs to the bedroom was built by Filipino carpenters who painstakingly beat the stainless steel by hand.

Right The bright red egg chair—a classic by designer Arne Jacobsen—is a bold presence among the cool and translucent glass panels and linear aluminium frames of the Sys' modernist dwelling.

Left Architectural elements, such as the installation under the skylight, are the main decorative features of the space. Furnishing is minimal. The bright oil painting by a young Philippine artist stands upright on a movable frame stand.

Below This cross section of the Sy house reveals the new modernist unit under the original 1980s bungalow roof.

Right An abstract design of four mirrors faces the traditional wooden front door at right. Beyond this stunning minimalist foyer is a series of sliding glass panels leading to the inner quarters.

oriented the "social zone" toward the rear, near to the swimming pool, which is set right up against the back fence. "Our lifestyle faces the back yard," says Sy, an IT dealer. "We have the outdoor greenery and pool in view, but there is no garden to take care of!" When guests do step out to view the façade of the "new" house, the old elevation is seen to the right, merged with the grid of steel and glass of the modernist insertion on the left.

Within the atrium, a metal plank staircase ascends to the mezzanine, from where one can look over a balcony to the living/dining/work area below. Bedrooms are small and cozy, their translucent sliding panels or lightweight walls all non-loadbearing and flexible so that they can be adjusted as the family grows! Most of the corridor walls, made of aluminum banding with translucent glass panes, are bent or "folded," for dynamic visual interest. "These folded walls allow natural light to creep into all corners," explains Yupangco. "This is a new way of interpreting architecture, one that is both ambiguous and flexible."

The designer has used a limited palette to exploit the contrast and juxtaposition of solid concrete with glass and metal. Materials shift from solid to transparent and from rectilinear to vertical, expressing an interesting dynamic between common building materials. Structural walls have been "cast in place"—a signature treatment of *beton brut* or raw concrete by the cutting-edge modernist: "The design derives from the process: we use architectural strategies to create shifts, skewing from conceived perceptions."

Everywhere sheet glass is widely used: as walls, cabinet panels, and large sliding doors. One expanse of frosted glazing hides a segmented wall closet, storing household belongings. All is neutral, without paint or color, reduced to silver, white, and metal gray from the sheen of steel and aluminum. Yupangco points proudly to the handcrafted workmanship on the spiraling steel stairway by the back. He explains, "Here the architecture is the artifact and the furnishing.... The house can stand with or without art because it's already an art form in itself."

Left An outdoor lounger by designer Richard Schultz complements the white portal frame of architect Ed Calma. The purist cubist house that Calma built opens up to views only of the South China Sea.

Right The rectilinear portals of "Bellavista" soar into the sky over the sea. The gap in the horizontal railing is a modernist twist to a cubist work.

knox house

"Architecture is not about style, it's about deriving a form from material technology. It's about original concepts. Architecture should be innovative and true to one's materials." EDUARDO CALMA

Josephine & Eirvin Knox

PUNTA FUEGO, NASUGBU, BATANGAS

ARCHITECT EDUARDO CALMA
LOR CALMA DESIGN, INC.

The upscale development of Punta Fuego in Nasugbu, Batangas, two and a half hours' drive from the chaos of Manila, comprises a number of prime rambling resort homes overlooking the South China Sea. Among them, cantilevered on a slope over the azure waters of Batangas, is an outstanding all-white concrete-and-glass structure. The pristine building, perched between earth, sea, and sky, resembles a stunning work of art, a cubist sculpture with flying buttresses and planar terraces.

International banking couple Josephine and Eirvin Knox commissioned Filipino designer Eduardo (Ed) Calma to build their retirement house, engaging the idealistic designer's passion for "Architecture with a capital A." It was a dream project on Philippine shores for Manila's up-and-coming young modernist, a graduate of the New York Pratt Institute and Columbia University.

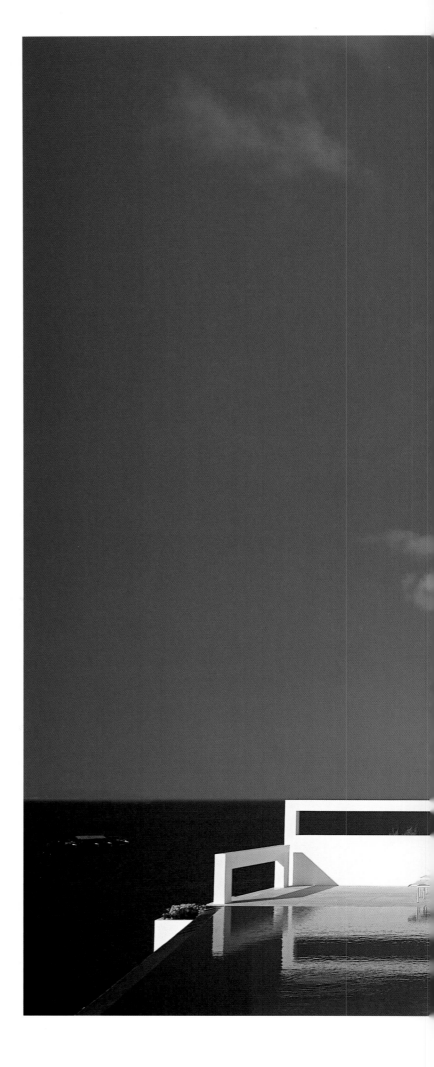

Josephine del Gallego-Knox says of her spectacular home: "This is a modernist Italian beach house, inspired by the white cliffside houses that dot the Mediterranean seascapes of Italy and Spain." The house, named "Bellavista" after her favorite Italian wine, had been simmering in her mind for as long as she can remember until, with the aid of Calma, it finally came to fruition in 2003.

The location of the Knox house was a challenge to the architect. The 1000-square meter property stands high on a rugged cliff, exposed to both tropical storms and fierce winds. Regardless, Calma chose to build the cubist house in glass and concrete. Four rectilinear "portals" soar up to the sky, while three terraces are cantilevered toward the sea. Picture glass curtain walls open all the main rooms to the ocean side of the house. There, horizontal white railings "float" to barely outline the tiled terraces, or rise to "frame" private views of the seamless ocean. A trapezoidal-shaped infinity pool on the edge of the main level complements the azure hue of the sea, while a low white terrace juts out over the water, forming a perfect place for enjoying evening cocktails.

Calma muses: "The Knox house is a multilevel house which responds to the slope of the site. It starts out as a modular mass at the entrance level, designed for privacy, and gradually opens up fully to frame views of the South China Sea. The site is deep with a narrow frontage. The multilevel solution allows each space to be organized along the broad length of the site to have views of the sea ... and nothing else."

"Bellavista" is awesome, inside and out, its purist form designed with an instinctive awareness for orientation and ventilation. As the east–west axis is not ideal—the house receives a large amount of sunshine—Calma shifted the house's west volume toward the sea, to shade the balcony on the east volume from the afternoon sun. He also limited the use of glass, even though this is one of his favorite mediums, instead allowing for cross-ventilation through high-placed vents among the clerestory windows. High ceilings also allow heat to rise and exit, while the cooler air circulates low over the sleek all-white furnishings by B&B Italia and Boffi.

Josephine Knox and Ed Calma collaborated closely for over two years to produce the Punta Fuego showcase. The Manila-based designer and his jet-setting client, who was an exacting project manager, pushed their mutual

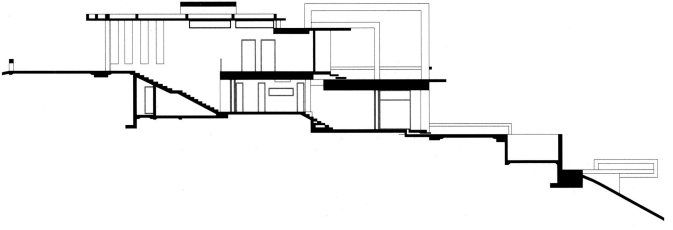

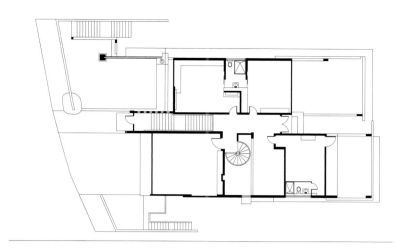

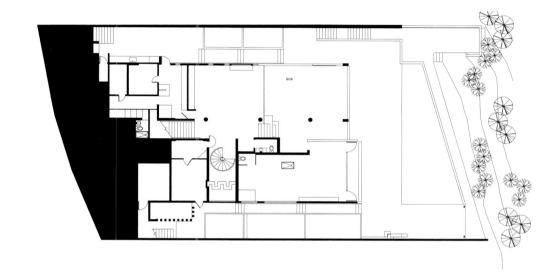

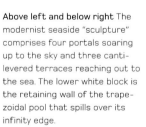

Above left and below right The modernist seaside "sculpture" comprises four portals soaring up to the sky and three cantilevered terraces reaching out to the sea. The lower white block is the retaining wall of the trapezoidal pool that spills over its infinity edge.

Left This longitudinal section reveals how the house is cantilevered on a slope. A small terrace at the lowest level, beyond the pool, juts out over the sea.

Above right The street level (top) and lower level (bottom) plans.

Left and above An indoor courtyard complements the minimalist spiral staircase leading to the guest rooms. The built-in vertical water feature (left), outlined with fiberoptic lights that change color, cascades down into an indented floor, a design inspired by an Australian garden magazine. An early nineteenth-century Mon pottery jar from Burma sits on a pedestal in the corner. The glass art pieces inset in the wall (above) are from Arcade, Italy, and are called "Zen."

Right Calma is proud of the asymmetry of the stairs, where he interplays materials: bleached white oak planks from Canada with painted 12-mm bent metal plates as railing.

Above left "Bellavista" allows an intriguing view of the Punta Fuego sunset (left), reflected on the large picture glass on the west-side setback. The owner's favorite spot (center) is the "Sunset Terrace," cantilevered over the sea. White outdoor furniture by Schulz is designed to cope with high winds! The onyx-tiled swimming pool (right) merges with the Batangas seas while horizontal elements provide "viewing frames" for the seascapes of boats and isles beyond the terrace.

Below left The master bedroom glows by night, as interior lights shine out from a sophisticated transparent closet system. The private suite enjoys an exclusive view of the infinity-edge pool and the sea.

Right With its all-glass counter and basin, and installation art, the powder room makes a chic minimalist statement.

Below The all-white dining room looks out over an azure blue seascape. Interior furnishings are exclusively B&B Italia and Boffi.

Left "Bellavista"'s portals on a long, shadowed afternoon. The eastern volume of the house is pushed back a few meters to allow the western volume to shade it from hot afternoon sun.

Below The façade bears elements from Josephine Knox's favorite designers: seven vertical slit openings from Ricardo Legoretta, a concrete water spout from Luis Barragan, and a sensuous white fiberglass chaise from Yushioko.

Right Viewed from the side, "Bellavista" steps down the steep slope. The house opens up exclusively to the sea, allowing no glimpses of its neighbors on either side.

Below right Even the setback has been carefully designed. The vertical row of white concrete elements, mirroring the seven tall slat windows on the façade, camouflage the air-conditioning units.

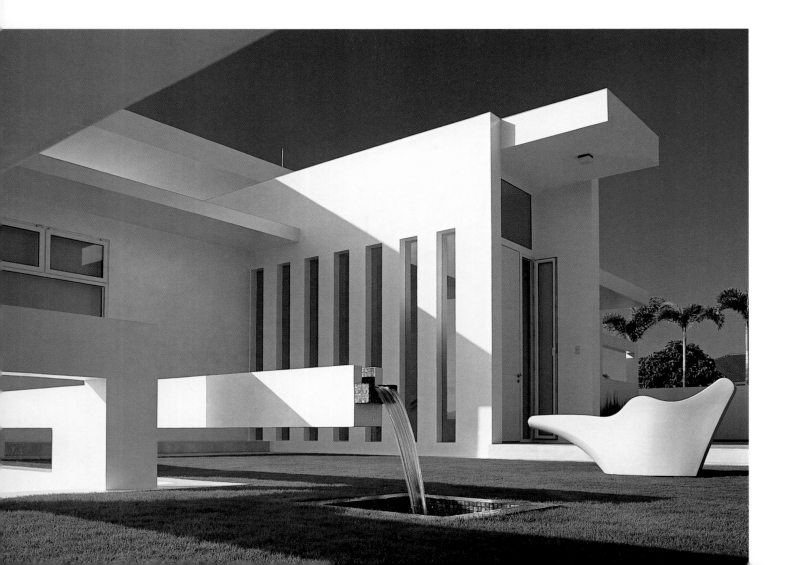

passion for architecture to the limit. She was the instigator, full of ideas and images of the type of architecture she loves. "Bellavista" thus contains influences adapted from her favorite modern architects: a white cantilevered fence imbedded in a giant boulder from Gae Aulenti and John Lautner; smooth white masonry from Richard Meier; seven tall vertical slit openings from her Mexican idol, Ricardo Legoretta; and concrete modernist water spouts from Luis Barragan. All details are beautifully merged in the gleaming sculptural work of Eduardo Calma.

Josephine Knox, though perhaps still dreaming of Italy, thoroughly enjoys her minimalist modernist house perched on a rise, while waiting for husband Eirvin to retire to Punta Fuego, Batangas. She relishes every waking moment in her dream house, catching the glow of sunrise when the house awakes, and the superb sea views. Architect Ed Calma reflects on the high-profile project by the sea: "The Knox house is like a camera that opens up to the light.... The architect shouldn't provide just the basic needs. He should provide a dwelling that uplifts the spirit, that makes one feel excited. To me, that's what architecture is about."

Left The Ngo house is an edgy creation on a massive scale. The imposing structure comprises a great grid of glass, enfolded by a sculpture of concrete. The giant lightbox cantilevered over the entry is both canopy and "lantern."

Right The bright and seamless dining area is an organic space under sloping ceilings that mirror the rolling land outside. The great atrium steps down to this single-story height and focuses on the greenery beyond the glass.

ngo house

"Architecture to me is about freedom ... to be free to animate, beyond conceived perceptions, an architectural event that articulates the relation of metaphysical behavior with time and space.... This project seeks to realize the abstract concepts of kinetics and circulation, as expressed in a structure of flexible living spaces." JOEY YUPANGCO

Edwin & Alice Ngo

AYALA HEIGHTS, QUEZON CITY, METRO MANILA

ARCHITECT JOEY YUPANGCO
JY+A

Ayala Heights, a subdivision built on the uneven terrain of Quezon City, is noted for its wide streets and massive bungalows set against a backdrop of grassy fields and rolling hills. The Ngo house—a modernist glass and concrete "sculpture" newly built in the conventional subdivision— is stopping people in their tracks.

An awkward site was just one of the challenges facing architect Joey Yupangco. In defiance of the principles of Chinese *fengshui*, the 700-square meter trapezoidal lot is located at a T-junction facing a down-sloping road, and is edged by a small creek at the rear. Another challenge was the task of convincing his clients that his experimental work—an expression of "process" rather than conventional beauty—was truly worth building. The architect sought to

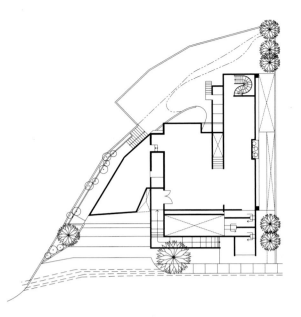

Left The ground floor plan shows how the architect worked within the limitations of a trapezoidal lot bordered by a small creek.

Below The back terrace is cantilevered over the small creek on the perimeter of the lot. The dining room at left extends over the large *koi* pond at the rear, its glass-bottomed floor allowing views of the fish below.

Bottom Longitudinal section of the Ngo house.

Right This interim space leading off the sunken garage has concrete walls wrapped in a black grid of steel, a pocket garden, and a large aquarium window for viewing the deep end of the fish pond.

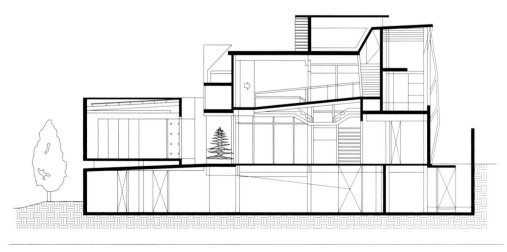

design a dynamic context for "spontaneous living" and a structure for "pushing forward the art of architecture." By luck or hubris, Yupangco's ideas were accepted by his clients, Edwin and Alice Ngo, restaurateurs and good friends, who then watched in amazement as the modernist structure rose on their lot.

The Ngo house is an edgy creation on a massive scale. The imposing façade is a giant grid of clear and translucent glass panels, enfolded on one end with a hood-like sculptural mass of bare, unpainted concrete. Visible through the glass façade, the interior is crossed diagonally by long, elevated ramps, on which people can pass from one side to the other at the higher level. An outdoor ramp leads to the front entry, while a giant hollow cube cantilevered over the front door serves as both a portico and a modern "lantern."

A fish pond alongside the entry ramp continues underground to be viewed as an aquarium from within the basement. The house's multiple-car garage is a massive sunken space with no doors.

Stepping into the house is like entering a glass and concrete sculpture of unorthodox planes and spaces. There are no rectilinear rooms in the Ngo house: every space is "irregular" in shape, and approached by unusual passages and corridors. Throughout the house, there are long ramps, overhead walkways or bridges, sloping floors, and bent ceilings. In certain areas, the plane of the floor slants slightly upward to meet a glass window, while over another area the ceiling dips down in a gentle V shape. The designer explains that the structure is "organically" related to the environs, mirroring the rolling landscape outdoors.

Left The master suite comprises unpainted but articulated walls and ceilings and inserted windows that interplay clear and translucent panes. A sheep stands sentinel in a loft which can be used for sleeping, storing things, or as a dressing room.

Right Concrete corridors lead to functional but flexible spaces. This narrow hall allows a glimpse of the minimalist kitchen, with its marble island, and the entrance to the spiral stairway to the basement.

The grand central interior is bright with natural light streaming in from all sides. Translucent glass provides a certain amount of privacy to the occupants at the ground level, while clear glass in selectively placed tall slot windows allows views of the street and neighborhood from the inside. Upstairs, one sees Yupangco's signature "folded" walls: concrete structural walls, which are poured on site into angled forms. Folded walls are created manually and painstakingly to articulate the entry of light and to serve as ornamentation for the structure.

According to Yupangco, the Ngo house is a "treatise" about *circulation*: the movement of air, light, and people within flexible living spaces. He says that three separate families could live together in the Ngo house, modifying the uses of the functional spaces. Taking his inspiration

Left The bedroom is an outré setting amid "folded" walls, uneven glass windows, and gently sloping floors. Yupangco's signature folded walls are structural constructs poured on site into angled forms.

Right A view of the sky through rails and banisters, glass and steel. Architect Yupangco allows for glazed transparency between the Ngo house's cutting-edge volumes.

Below Concrete steps also serve as graphic design. From the cool concrete kitchen, the circular staircase spirals down into the shadows of the basement.

from the new European modernism espoused by the main proponents Rem Koolhaas and Philippe Starck, Yupangco challenges the common notion that a house is a static thing; he discards traditional concepts of space and form in order to break new ground for contemporary architecture. To him, every space is flexible, mutable, changing its function or identity to meet the needs of the occupants. The Ngo house thus represents a new way of thinking, viewing, and living in a flexible space.

In terms of construction methods and materials, the Ngo house also breaks architectural ground. Ordinary materials like cement and glass are manipulated in unexpected ways on site, demonstrating the completely manual construction of a modernist structure. As the designer eschews superficial ornamentation, the hands-on building *process* itself—using low-end technology and basic building fundamentals under close supervision—overrides common assumptions of "beauty."

Yupangco concludes: "The house will definitely grow from its original concept, as the occupants are free to change the spaces, thus making it dynamic.... Architecture does not end with the architect's work; rather, the architecture lives on as its users shape and are shaped by it."

Al & Carla Tengco

FORBES PARK, MAKATI CITY, METRO MANILA

DESIGNERS BUDJI LAYUG & ROYAL PINEDA
BUDJI LAYUG+ROYAL PINEDA DESIGN ARCHITECTS

tengco townhouse

"Modern style is manifested in sleek, sophisticated lines and cutting-edge design,
regardless of the space available. Our challenge was to renovate an old Mediterranean
townhouse in Makati, to expand the space in appearance and size while achieving
sophistication, coziness, and timelessness."   BUDJI LAYUG

In this remarkable transformation of a 1980s townhouse,
design partners Budji Layug and Royal Pineda have mas-
tered the limitations of a small urban house, a cramped,
high-density site, and restrictive building regulations. The
result is a modern white dwelling, a visual and spatial
delight that stands out from the rustic townhouses which
surround it. For home owners Al and Carla Tengco, the
greatest achievement of the restoration lies in the homey,
sophisticated interior beyond the streamlined façade.

In this renovation project, the architects have successfully combined a picturesque "modern Mediterranean"
vision, an expanded space solution, and a sensory play
of interior details. For the exterior, they opted for clean,
modern, and simple lines, with the limited frontage forming a stately presence. The façade, composed of white
planes and floating slabs, enhanced by a single mature tree,

forms a poetic composition in contrast to the gardens of
neighboring houses. The all-white front elevation now
includes clear railings around balconies, glass canopy overhangs (to let in light), and an inspired raised rooftop "that
opens up like an envelope flap!" Tropical wood, set against
smooth white outer walls, is used to frame doors and
windows, evoking Layug's concept of "Tropical Modern."

The interior of the Tengco townhouse is a fusion of
innovative devices for space expansion, contemporary materials, and intriguing design ideas, all combined to achieve
the desired modern Mediterranean look. Judicious cuta-
ways of the original walls visually expand the living space
outward, through picture glass, to the white wall bordering
the lot. The living and entertaining areas on the ground
floor exploit the landscape features. All interior walls are
painted white to highlight the house's design features and

the owners' fine art collection and contemporary furniture.

Sculptural staircases are a hallmark of Layug's interiors. In the entry foyer, which is lined in light gray tile, a dark-stained "floating" stairway suggestive of an accordion, that turns an L-corner mid-air before touching ground, forms both a welcoming statement and a strong graphic impression. The stairway is placed over a shallow reflecting pool that continues to the outside. A picture window at the side looks out to the pool and to a bamboo garden.

The adjoining living and dining areas comprise an expansive tiled space demarcated by a floating horizontal console. The elegantly appointed *sala* or living room is set under a cantilevered floor, opening up two corners of the house to the perimeter of the property. Huge sliding glass doors frame views of the greenery outside, while sunlight dances through bamboo grass in the manner of Oriental paintings. A narrow water feature that begins outside the foyer area continues outside the living room area, defining and unifying a wraparound landscape.

Frosted and clear glass have been used to maximum effect. The powder room on the ground floor, located beneath the wooden stairs, is a boldly designed frosted glass cubicle with a clear glass washbasin built into an all-glass countertop. Upstairs, the use of a fully mirrored hallway leading to the bedrooms conjures up a spacious feeling in a passage lit by sunlight through large glazed openings. A second staircase leading up to the attic is both sculptural and "see through"; accordion steps ascend the wall with voids in place of risers.

The transformed third-level attic is the favorite room of the Tengcos. Once a forgotten space used for sundry storage, it has been converted into a spacious and flexible open-plan family lounge and entertainment area. Large triangulated windows, sliding glass doors, and frosted partitions allow views of the outside. The raised "envelope flap" portion of this upper floor leads to a viewing terrace, where one can gaze down on the crowded urban landscape from the level of the trees.

Left The adjoining living/dining areas comprise a seamless space demarcated by a floating horizontal console. The *sala* has glazed picture windows and cantilevered corners that visually expand the space to the outer walls of the lot.

Below The once-neglected third-level attic was transformed into a popular family room. Large triangulated windows, sliding glass doors, and frosted glass partitions allow views of the outside at the level of the trees and rooftops.

Bottom The designer stairway, suggestive of an accordion, turns a corner mid-air before touching ground by the entry. An unusual water feature runs from the foyer to the peripheral wall, then along the outside toward the *sala* area.

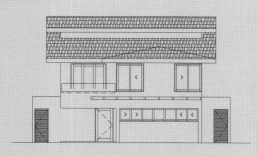

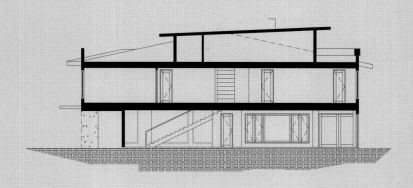

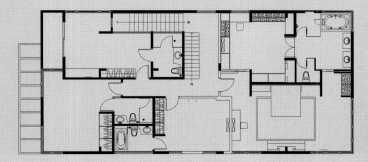

Left All interior walls are painted white to visually expand the space as well as to highlight the owners' fine collection of art. The art gallery in the foyer displays a stone sculpture by Impy Pilapil and an abstract painting by Gus Albor.

Above The front elevation (top), longitudinal section (center), and ground floor plan (below) of the Tengco townhouse.

Above right A fully glassed wall conjures an immense spatial illusion. The staircase up to the third-level attic is also a sculptural work: "see-through" accordion steps ascend the structural wall with voids in place of risers.

Right A glass canopy hangs over the picture windows in the bordering setback, protecting the interior from rain without blocking the light. A lighted "moat" defines the wraparound landscape.

montinola pavilions

"A large 'serenity program' called for a house that breathes; an airy and serene setting.... Here is asymmetry expressed in a free-flowing plan, and transparency seen through a scaled horizontality.... Here among pavilions around a courtyard will begin a series of family stories, interconnected...."

ANDY LOCSIN

ROMEO DELFINADO & ANDY LOCSIN

Home owner Gizela Montinola asked for a "living, breathing house with a serene ambience and a peaceful Zen air, where she could commune with nature…, a tactile and textured house where man and nature would interact … where there is the feeling of rain on wet stone and rooms that slide into one another…."

The architects responded to both the home owner's "serenity program" and to her wish to preserve four trees on the site, in particular a magnificent old *narra* at the front, by creating an asymmetrical grouping of free-flowing pavilions around a broad courtyard. The well-modulated spaces on the spacious site feel comfortable, not intimidating, as they grow and flow together. There is abundant spirit and transparency amid the house's horizontality, along with serene, framed views across the open-ended courtyard of water pools, rock gardens, and lush garden greenery.

Aurelio III & Gizela Montinola

FORBES PARK, MAKATI CITY, METRO MANILA

ARCHITECTS ROMEO DELFINADO & ANDY LOCSIN
LEANDRO V. LOCSIN PARTNERS, ARCHITECTS

Above At night, the century-old *narra* tree lording it over the family's private courtyard is reflected in the pool lining the meditation pavilion at left. An asymmetrical grouping of three pavilions, representing the head, body, and tail of a "dragon," is placed around the broad lawn.

Above left The ancient *narra* tree is the focal point of the front entrance to the house. From inside the courtyard, the tree is visible over the low yellow corridor wall linking the house's three pavilions.

Left The starkness of the wall on the courtyard side is softened by a single vertical viewing slot and a rock and sand garden. Outdoor lighting by specialist lighting designer Tina Periquet adds a magical touch in the evening.

Above The meditation pavilion, closely underlined by the swimming pool, appears to visually float on its blue waters. Dressed in *shoji* screens and *tatami* mats, it is a peaceful retreat embraced by water elements.

Right The wood-encased windows of the Japanese-style meditation pavilion frame serene views of the reflective pond, the swimming pool, and colonnaded walkways.

Left The dining room, designed by Yola Johnson, expresses a Japanese sensibility. Fine upholstery fabric, a Venetian lamp, and an antique *obi* table runner blend with rustic Roman shades made of native Philippine *buntal*.

Below left The wood-lined staircase landing is lit by natural light through wood-framed windows. Hugging the wall of the staircase are Japanese-inspired modular storage cabinets by wood artist Claude Tayag.

Below right The white-pebbled setback area holds a Zen garden alongside the open corridor. "It is a tactile house with lots of different textures," says the owner.

Right The *sala*, a collaboration by designers Yola Johnson and Fernando Ocampo, displays Asian allusions, from the low quiet furniture to the picture window overlooking a *bonsai* garden.

The first challenge facing the architects was to incorporate the century-old *narra* as the centerpiece of the house's design and to build around the other trees on the site. The house could not be wrapped around the *narra* up front, as there was inadequate setback from the property line. The solution was to build a low linking wall *behind* the tree—much like a spirit wall—connecting the pavilions at both ends. Viewed from within the compound, with this sleek corridor wall as foreground, the great *narra* tree looms framed and "embraced" by the pavilions on its flanks and the watery courtyard.

The overall plan includes three distinct pavilions in a classic U-shaped head-to-tail configuration, reminiscent of the "dragon" form in traditional Chinese architecture. The main two-story structure of family quarters and social spaces, which soars to a two-story atrium ceiling over an indoor–outdoor *lanai*, comprises the "head" of the dragon. Attached to the other end of the low linking wall is the single-story office pavilion, and at right angles to that, connected by a colonnaded walkway, is a Japanese-style meditation pavilion, which appears to float on the large, rippling swimming pool.

The integration of water elements, architectural detailing, and landscaping reflects the Asian concerns of the architects, Romeo Delfinado and Andy Locsin, and of the Locsin firm as a whole, as well as the distinctively Japanese

Zen sensibility of the lady of the house, Gizela Montinola. "The overall idea of the house," says Locsin, "is to accommodate a large program without it appearing intimidating ... to frame serene views of the house from every angle, while looking across water as the central focal point ... and provide a dramatic experience through the sequential and spatial planning of the home.

"The pavilion scheme is now very popular and versatile, giving the feeling of a community within a private compound.... We can vary the functions of rooms later; the office pavilion can be converted into a granny flat when needed. The separate units allow one to view the other parts from afar.... Here will begin a series of family stories, interconnected...." Exterior walls facing the central garden are treated as a series of sliding planes in varying degrees of transparency, while views from the second floor are framed by cantilevered corner windows.

Today, the Montinola couple love the serenity of their home. Gizela reflects: "It is a tactile house with lots of different textures, including yellow sandstone that will show its weathering.... We hear the wind in the trees and the rippling waters. The house is never static; it shows the interplay between man and nature, the rain on wet stone and grass and plants growing.... The big old *narra* tree sheds its leaves in winter, and we watch time and the seasons shift around the house."

Below The connecting corridor to the meditation pavilion comprises a procession of solid wood columns set on round concrete bases. The subtle curve of the ceiling gives the illusion of a splayed roof.

Bottom The front (left) and rear (right) elevations of the house.

Right The owner's meditation room has a peaceful Zen air. The room is enclosed by sliding *shoji* screens, its floors covered with *tatami* mats. To the front, the pavilion looks out over the waters of the reflective pool, and on the other side, to lush gardens landscaped by Jun Obrero.

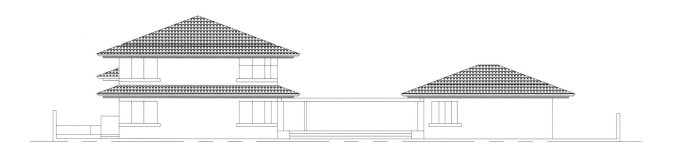

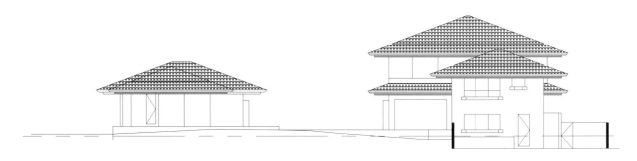

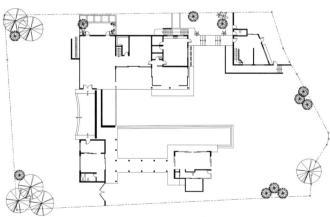

Top The narrow vertical slot in the stark dividing wall at the main entrance allows a peek into the courtyard garden behind.

Above The ground floor plan of the house shows the juxtaposition of the three linked pavilions.

Right Serene mantras emit from the pavilion reflected in the pool's waters. The Montinola house is open to the sounds of the wind and the rain—and the "interplay between man and nature."

VALLE VERDE, PASIG, METRO MANILA

ARCHITECT EDUARDO CALMA
LOR CALMA DESIGN, INC.

atrium house

"I believe in architecture that is formed by the uniqueness of the site, the clients' brief, the clients themselves, and the situation. I try to clarify an idea by subtracting what is not necessary to the form until it has been reduced to the essentials." EDUARDO CALMA

Left Entry to the Atrium house is on the north by the perimeter wall, along an alleyway adjoining an all-white pebbled one-meter-wide easement that lets in light. From the front door one can see right up to the third level of the house—and to the sky.

Above The double-height *sala* is given grandeur by minimal elements: modular furniture in neutral shades of gray from Bo Concepts, and a large abstract painting in multiple tones and textures by young artist Lindslee.

The Atrium house is located in a typical 1970s suburban enclave adjacent to the Ortigas Center, one of Metropolitan Manila's outlying business districts. The thoroughly modern module sits at the base of an escarpment that slopes down to the Pasig River. Views of the spectacular skyline of Ortigas can be enjoyed from the third-story terrace of the house.

Designed by the Philippine's leading modernist architect, Eduardo (Ed) Calma, the house is "a response to an urban environment that has become visually chaotic and security compromised. Its garden and views have been turned inward to the central atrium-cum-modern white courtyard—where light and wind are filtered."

From the street, the structure appears as a giant white box articulated with overlapping concrete envelopes that allow light and air to enter through long, narrow openings. The front elevation is clad with a solid slab of sandstone that highlights the façade's asymmetry. Entry is via the long entrance alleyway at the side of the house, since a

fengshui requirement dictated that access to the house be on the northern side of the lot.

The entire house is introverted, its exterior shell making full use of the 425-square meter lot, right up to the boundary walls. This introversion is strikingly expressed in the three-level structure whose living spaces are organized around a nine-meter-high atrium enclosed by a translucent polycarbonate ceiling! Two eucalyptus trees provide colorful accents in the all-white atrium, at the same time highlighting just how large this space is. Linear window slots allow northern light to filter in and also provide the occupants with glimpses of the pebbled strip that forms an abstract "garden-path" all around the house.

A glass wall separates the atrium from the double-height living room, which continues down to the one-story dining nook. The glass partitions enclosing all rooms allow views of spaces within spaces as well as the domestic activities within.

A grand staircase is the main focus of the atrium, its steel diagonal lines and *guiho* wood railings dramatizing the central volume. Four flights of stairs lead to wide balconies between rooms, and finally to the highest level, the terrace—giving the atrium the feeling of a small apartment building with a private plaza below.

Bedrooms occupy the second floor, with the master and guest bedrooms looking down on the atrium. The

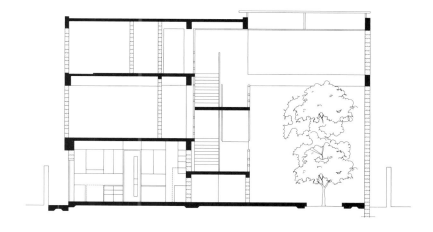

Above The interior is soaring and bright. A glass partition wall separates the six-meter-high *sala* from the nine-meter-high atrium/ courtyard. Stylized louvers in the *sala* filter in light from the surrounding garden-path.

Above right Section view of the Atrium house.

Right The entire house looks inward to the atrium/courtyard. Window slots allow northern light to filter into the house while giving scale and composition to the modernist environment, centered by two eucalyptus trees.

Above The atrium gives rise to the sculptural staircase, its diagonal lines dramatizing the upward sweep of the central volume. Four flights of stairs lead to three levels of glazed spaces stacked over the courtyard below.

Right The lofty view three floors above the all-white courtyard. The translucent polycarbonate roofing over the atrium allows sunlight to penetrate the interior, while the open-air terrace permits ventilation from above.

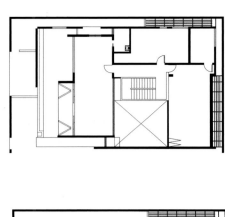

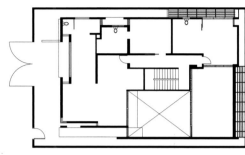

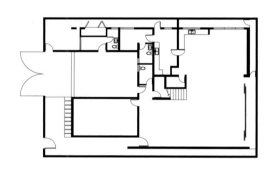

Above From bottom to top, the ground, second, and third floor plans of the Atrium house.

Right The open-sided roofed terrace on the west side of the house forms a modern ventilation deck, allowing air to flow directly into the central atrium while dissipating heat from inside. Two yellow Pantone fiberglass chairs harmonize with the house's purist scheme.

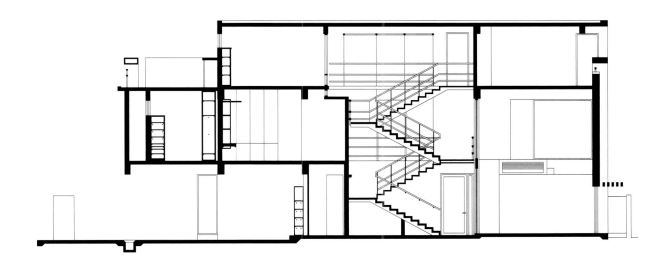

Left Frank Gehry's iconic Wiggle chair takes pride of place by the pivoted doors of the upper terrace. Since moving into the house, the young owners have been scouting for modern designer chairs to fill the great expanse.

Above From the street, the house is a giant white box articulated with overlapping envelopes of concrete and long, narrow interstitial spaces for light and air. The entire house is introverted, filtering selective views to the outside.

Below East elevation of the house.

third floor contains two areas at either end of the stairwell corridor: a library and a work room on the east side and a large open-sided roofed terrace on the west, which allows sunset views of the business district's skyline. Both spaces have large, pivoted partitions that can be angled to adjust the amount of light and air flowing into the atrium.

Designer Calma states: "Cross-ventilation is maximized throughout the house when the partitions on the third-level terrace are opened to scoop in the wind and dissipate the heat from inside the house. It's a modern house that really works in a tropical environment."

Left A "tropical Georgian" façade is defined by four bold, round columns wrapped in Philippine *yakal* wood. The posts soar from a "five-foot way" to the wide-eaved roof—inspired by the archetypal Singapore shophouse.

Right The columned house makes a bold design statement over the surrounding fence. The basic box geometry reflects a graphic horizontality: black steel ledges act as sun screens, at the same time protecting awning-style windows.

Agot Isidro & Manuel Sandejas

ALABANG HILLS, MUNTINLUPA, METRO MANILA

ARCHITECT JEFF ISIDRO
THE AMPERSAND ARCHITECTS

isidro-sandejas house

"This is an eclectic house—my personal tribute to the typical Singapore shophouse. The front porch is like a "five-foot way," with the front door placed perfectly symmetrically between two framed windows. The façade is defined by four giant tropical columns and wide eaves; and makes a statement over the fence.... But inside, the traditional merges with a modern white space. Modern meets old-fashioned by the back stairwell, where a rounded wood banister meets stainless steel struts—and feels like Art Deco." JEFF ISIDRO

The owners of this home are two popular media figures, Agot Isidro of television, broadcast, and print, and Manuel Sandejas, creative head of a leading advertising agency. The well-traveled couple collects rustic wood furniture and sentimental ideas, especially from the Isidros's airy old family house in Marikina. As newlyweds, they had purchased an antique Chinese door, their first heirloom, and wanted a modern house planned around it. Their brief to the architect was for a "simple, very square, open, and easy house that was Asian-inspired," a practical home, rustic yet modern, designed to allow tropical light and ventilation to enter throughout.

The architect, Agot's brother Jeff Isidro, had spent eight years in Singapore preserving and retrofitting buildings. He had brought home to Manila the cultural image of "those wonderful shophouses," where Chinese families ply their trade on the sidewalk and conduct their lives in the back yard. "So this is my personal tribute to the Singaporean

shophouse!" says Isidro, "a modern interpretation of the terrace house ... almost a subconscious effort on my part. Dare I call it architecture by osmosis?"

The shophouse—a fusion of the narrow, fronted houses of Amsterdam and the shop-homes of southern China—was adopted in Singapore in the nineteenth century. It was described as a house with "a uniform type of front verandah—open at all times as a covered passage on each side of the street." This semi-public verandah, later renamed the "five-foot way," was cared for by the house owner, but was shared by passers-by, plants, chairs, pets, and bicycles.

The Isidro-Sandejas house, located in suburban Alabang on the southern edge of Metro Manila, is a contemporary interpretation of the shop, terrace, or row house. The façade is strongly defined by a tropical colonnade formed of four bold, round columns wrapped in Philippine *yakal* wood, set on stone bases, which soar from the "covered sidewalk" to the wide-eaved roof. Windows straddle the central door.

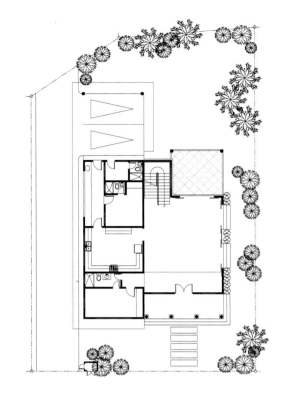

The grand scale gives the house a "tropical Georgian" air, while broadcasting a distinctive statement to the Alabang neighborhood, courtesy of Isidro and his co-designing partner Ramon Santelices.

The house's box-like geometry is articulated with fenestrations—black steel "ledges" which act as partial sun screens while protecting awning-style glass windows—that contribute to the house's graphic horizontality. Despite the tall colonnade up front, the house remains human-scaled and friendly, aided by the familiar five-foot way treatment of the pedestrian entry. The front porch is styled in wood and crazy-cut *araal* stone as part of the designers' geometric modernist approach.

Entry is through the antique Chinese door, now set in an architrave. Inside, the traditional "shophouse" merges with a relaxed, all-white home, visually expanded with an airwell-cum-lightwell, which forms a double-height volume over the foyer. This "lantern" of reflected natural light affects the spatial quality of the interior, dramatizing its utilitarian nature. The space then unrolls seamlessly from entry to rear, linking modern *sala* to dining area to *lanai* and back garden. The décor is eclectic, arranged by Agot herself, and comprises a mixture of rustic Cordilleran or lowland pieces and artifacts from regional Asian travels.

Opposite above left The two-story lightwell "lantern" in the entrance provides enough natural light during the day that no artificial lighting is needed. White walls contribute to the light, airy feel. The old Chinese door was the couple's first heirloom purchase: the house was built around it!

Opposite above right Ground floor plan.

Left The Art Deco-inspired stairway mixes materials: a curved wood banister, stainless steel struts, metal wire rails, and black steel ledges for sun screening.

Top The casually open *sala* features an eclectic mix of elements for a relaxed Asian lifestyle: ethnic furniture, a five-piece sofa by Vico Inc., and cultural artifacts.

Above Front elevation.

Another modern feature is the glazed stairwell leading to the upstairs. On the landing at the back of the stairwell, a ground-to-ceiling wall of black steel ledges and awning windows lets in sunlight and air. Isidro says, "The open stairwell is where modern meets old-fashioned again ... a curved wood banister meets stainless steel struts—and feels Art Deco." In fact, most of the house's design interest is created through the selection of a variety of materials: natural wood columns, horizontal steel windows, off-white tiled floors, wood plank steps, rustic furnishings, and a comfy modular sofa set.

The square geometry of the main house is countered at the back by a two-vehicle garage which intrudes on the back yard, at the same time forming an enclosure for the deep, square terrace which extends out from the *sala*. From the terrace, one looks out on an ample lawn and to the garden planted along the perimeter wall. The corners of the terrace feature squat wooden columns, which echo the thematic "Georgian" columns at the front of the house. Two triangular carved wooden panels attached to the top of each column add a Muslim accent: "That represents our quarter heritage that's Palestinian," says architect Isidro. The eclectic mix of modern elements and cultural expressions gel well with the owners' casual Asian lifestyle.

Top Stony paths and a variety of tropical plants wrap around the house, up to the spacious grass yard by the *lanai*. The home owners deliberately chose the most distinctive varieties to plant in the side setbacks.

Above The open-air *lanai*, where indoors meets outdoors on an *araal* stone patio, is the owners' favorite lounging place. Two more wood columns bear ornate corner-details—"carved elements honoring our Muslim heritage."

JEFF ISIDRO

Right The window treatment combines awning-style glass panels below the window sill and wood blinds above it—an allusion to the *ventanillas* (little windows) of traditional Philippine wood houses.

Below The *lanai* is where the home owners entertain at night—complete with vigil candles for atmosphere. The simple square geometry of the house is accompanied by a separate volume forming the garage, at right.

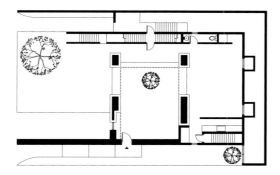

pedrosa courtyard house

"Architecture is ... the making and preserving of space: space of depth and energy; space that is full; space that can be felt. Those that inhabit it—people, objects, flowers—are given presence: presence through contrast and the reduction of elements to a minimum. Elements at their most fundamental ... a tree, or a chair, or the sky ... are set against bare, unadorned walls. Eye and mind are not distracted by superfluous decorations and are set free to perceive more purely." MARTA PEDROSA

Alfonso & Carmen N. Pedrosa

ALABANG HILLS, MUNTINLUPA, METRO MANILA

ARCHITECT MARTA PEDROSA

Left Treading an unusual path, home owner Carmen Navarro Pedrosa ascends the monolith's amazing dual staircase installed between the structural walls. Thirty-three steps climb in a graphic V formation from the ground to the third floor!

Above left Ground floor plan.

Above right The mango-colored monolith is a cubic volume with tiny square windows and no roof over the courtyard. The big bold block is adapted from a traditional house of the desert.

One of the most striking houses in Hillsborough, Alabang, an upscale subdivision south of Manila, is an austere rectangular block pierced by tiny windows. Passers-by label it the "big yellow cube," or "that Barragan house in Hillsborough." It has been variously called a smuggler's haven, a mortuary, and a birdcage. Those who understand architecture take a second look and say, "What a beautiful house!"

The yellow monolith, sitting solidly in stark contrast to its conventional suburban neighbors, is bold, disciplined, and graphic. It was designed as a "celebration" of the tropical sun and sky by a Filipino architect trained in Britain. The daughter of journalist Carmen Navarro Pedrosa, who writes scathing columns from within the monolith, Marta Pedrosa would spend idyllic summers in the Philippine provinces while she was growing up, experiencing the tropical environment. Conceived as a project that challenged the eye and mind and honored the "dominant sky," the new Pedrosa home was built in 1998. As the young

architect explained: "For me, the sky was something to be celebrated, its beauty to be focused upon and enhanced."

Pedrosa's first major work was blessed with perfect clients, her parents, who gave her total freedom to do as she liked. The resulting massive but minimalist family abode is a purist work of art that explores the "intensity and variety of the daylight, the fast and relentless strength of the rainfall." As Marta reassured her parents at the time, "Design begins with the first reaction to the site and surroundings; even before the pragmatics of the brief. All decisions flow from the distillation of the response....You will only see the virtue of the house when you live in it.... Any journey up or down or along a hallway becomes an intense spatial and sensory experience."

The lines of the Pedrosa house are indeed severe, minimalist, and unembellished. Its color is bright and bold, like archetypal Luis Barragan. The house takes its influence from Marta's one-time mentor Claudio Silvestrin, a leading minimalist architect in London, whose credo is as pristine as that of the master Mies van der Rohe: "Less is more." Despite the architect's purist bent, the typology of the Pedrosa home is, in fact, adapted from a traditional model: the adobe house of the hot/dry Middle Eastern desert. From Morocco to Tunisia, thick-walled, flat-topped homes are built to cope with abundant sun and heat and little rain. Distinctive features of the Pedrosa tropical adaptation are the placement of windows high up on the façade and the inclusion of spy-holes and ventilation openings; the shady courtyard; and the rooftop where the occupants can retreat after sundown. Like the typical adobe house, the Pedrosa courtyard house features a double-wall system, which drives air through the interstices, called the Venturi cooling effect. The house's bright mango color also helps to reduce heat gained during the day.

The monolith was designed to be "enigmatic" and to elicit "appreciation and surprise when entering the courtyard." On the front elevation, a square spy-hole and the dark ramp going down to the basement car park are treated as sculptural embellishments on an otherwise plain façade. Once through the side door, the introverted façade opens up to a cobblestone courtyard, a kind of private park between apartment buildings. A lone tree and a stone bench stand among the four massive walls that soar skyward. Traditional spaces such as the living and dining areas and the kitchen open directly off the courtyard at ground level, all facing inward to the center. The theme remains Pedrosa's dominant sky: the sunlight overhead qualifies the angled light and shadows through the day, like a sundial over a hollow space. The high walls provide a giant frame for viewing the sky and a focus for the inhabitants. The designer explains: "The enclosure captures the intensity of light, shadow, and sky and is filled by the infinite depth of the night sky. It is a void, but the space is full—of sky."

Pedrosa muses on her minimalist leanings: "Contrast is the best way of enhancing and focusing the senses. A

Opposite A long tunnel skylight lights the library on the mezzanine floor, which spans the width of the house. Journalist Carmen Pedrosa works one level below, at the base of the additional bookshelves (right), on a series of tables lined up against the supporting wall.

Top The entrance in the far left corner stands near a one-meter square spy-hole which gives a view of the street. Although the courtyard house is "enigmatic" on the outside, the occupants inside can spot anyone who approaches.

Above From an ornate chair in the ground floor dining room, one has a "selective view" of sky and trees beyond the perimeter wall.

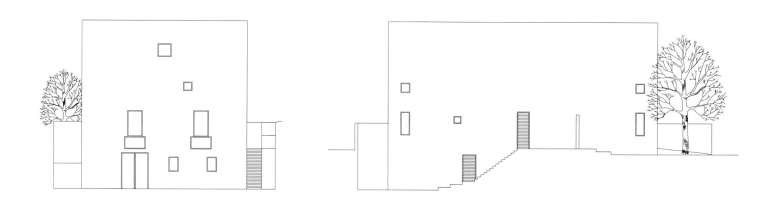

simple unadorned mass offers the perfect contrast to its surroundings. The meeting of the earth and sun is celebrated by a structure with sufficient sculptural presence to address both without being overwhelmed by either."

The monolithic structure contains six modest bedrooms on the two upper levels, with a continuous concrete balcony rimming the courtyard below. Every room has small "selected views" of sky and trees, and large inward views of the cobblestone courtyard and balconies opposite.

Finally, there is the house's most stunning interior feature: the dual staircase. Behind one massive full-height wall on one side of the courtyard are two mirror-image staircases, each 33 steps, facing each other in a giant V formation as they climb within the supporting walls—from the ground level straight to the third floor on either side! The long diagonal ascent toward the overhead skylight spells an "intense spatial and sensory experience"—just as Marta Pedrosa had assured her family it would. At the top of the monolith, the roof deck is ideal for viewing the neighborhood, for entertaining, and for star-gazing.

verandah house

"We design from the interior outward, favoring the courtyard form, where we can manipulate the space through compression and expansion. The goal is to create a separate world, isolated from the urban scene, and to duplicate the relaxed feeling of a resort so that you think you're at the beach!" MILO VAZQUEZ

MAKATI CITY, METRO MANILA

ARCHITECT MILO VAZQUEZ
VAZQUEZ & ASSOCIATES

Left Guests to the house are welcomed not by the usual foyer but by a wide U-shaped corridor elevated five steps over a small lawn. They cross this columned verandah to arrive at the living/dining pavilion at the opposite end.

Above Glass sculptures by Ramon Orlina are displayed on the inside wall adjoining the verandah. Light from three portholes enters the innovative shelving system.

When architect Milo Vazquez rebuilt his old family house in the crowded suburbs of Quezon City as a resort-like courtyard house to recall "the relaxed feeling of a resort," the house caught the attention of passers-by and won new clients who wanted a similar slice of his "separate world."

This new white residence in Makati City thus originated with a request for a courtyard-type Vazquez house "but with more modern touches." Working within a confined lot with height restrictions and walls on either side, and taking into account the clients' needs, the architect designed a C-shaped "footprint" which faces inward to a three-sided courtyard. The house includes a spacious basement below and an open deck on top.

The façade of the house is ultra "tropical modern" without being starkly minimalist. White and restrained, the fine, linear volume with its ash-shingled roof bears just one retro accent: giant gray-brown metal louvers placed at both levels on the front. This sunshade system, which alludes to

Below The interior of the house is the creative work of designer Joy Pimentel-Dominguez. Under its high, vaulted ceiling, the *sala* features tropical furnishing, eclectic Asian accents, and a mural by Ferdie Montemayor. The centerpiece is a huge baroque chandelier composed of sixteen alabaster globe lamps with aluminum swags.

Bottom The ground floor plan of the Verandah house.

Right Paired "raja" seats inside the entrance to the house provide a view across the U-shaped courtyard elevated over five steps to the *sala* pavilion with its distinctive pitched roof and raised floor, reminiscent of a Balinese *bale*.

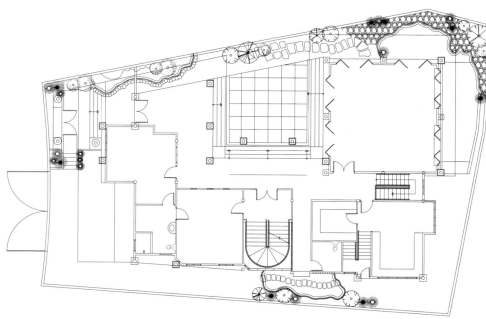

the wooden shutters of Singapore's colonial homes (a favorite detail of the home owner), can be adjusted mechanically to temper the tropical light or to let in breezes. Four peepholes on the façade lend an air of mystery, while the lack of large windows helps to deal with the afternoon sun that plagues that side of the house. Being highly conscious of Manila's tropical weather, the architect has made sure that the "house openings are all facing southeast—where the rain doesn't enter during the northwest winds. So instead ... one can *enjoy* the rain!"

In contrast to the white modernist exterior, the interior of the house is colorful, pan-Asian, and eclectic, infused with creative "surprises" by collaborating architect/designer Joy Pimentel-Dominguez. Guests enter the house through a rustic door paneled in beaten bamboo, to be greeted not by the usual foyer but by an open-air courtyard. On the far

end is a large airy pavilion with a distinctive Asian profile: a high-pitched roof and raised platform (an allusion to the Balinese *bale*) that drops down to the side lawn. This raised *sala*, which has foldaway doors on three sides, is the entertainment heart of the courtyard house. The Asian scheme features strong red accents in door frames and windows, blue lights along the floor, Art Deco or retro furnishings, rustic/ethnic wood details, and thoroughly individualistic accessories.

The L-shaped verandah leads also to the functional spaces on the ground floor: the front studio-office, a guest room, kitchen, living room, and stairs down to the large audiovisual den. The spaces flow easily one into the other. The two main spatial elements at this public level, the central courtyard and pavilion, are similar in area—seeming to mimic each other in an architectural *yin* and *yang*.

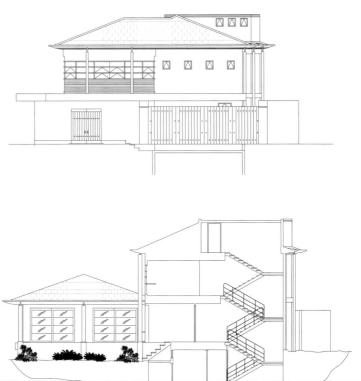

Above left Adjustable metal louvers at both levels of the house—inspired by the slatted shutters of Singapore's colonial homes—modulate light and air.

Above Front elevation (top) and cross section (bottom).

Left The separate *sala* pavilion, with its foldaway glass doors on three sides, smooth white columns, traditional extended eaves, and picturesque views across the inner courtyard, is the social hub of the Verandah house.

Above right The façade of the house is ultra "tropical modern" without being starkly minimalist. The fine linear volume, integrated with a clean white metal fence and ash-shingled roof, includes a basement and a third-level deck.

Below right The spiral staircase leading upstairs, secured within a glazed and pebbled stairwell behind sliding doors, is the home's showpiece. It is composed of solid *narra* planks and welded metal bars capped by a sinuous railing.

The bedroom level is accessed via a spiral staircase that is tucked away from public view by wide sliding doors. Behind these panels (veneered with "tiger wood") stands the architect's sculptural statement: a showpiece staircase in rich *narra* hardwood trimmed with welded metal bars. The stair base springs from a pebble-covered bed (which may be turned into a reflection pool one day). The solid plank steps grow wider as they rise, guided by a smooth, sensuous banister, and spiral twice around to the second and third levels.

Finally, at the top of the spiral steps, a flat roof deck atop the house contains the laundry area—a rather unorthodox but very practical concept! On fine tropical nights, the open deck doubles as the owners' private lounge and bar, where they entertain under the stars of Makati!

zobel rest house

"The desire to create an environment that's restful, peaceful, contemplative, and meditative; the desire for tranquility and harmony with nature ... is the sole influence in the materialization of this house. As the Japanese say, 'If you reduce everything to nature, it feels at home.'" NOEL M. SARATAN

Patsy Zobel & Alonso Halfttner

CALATAGAN, BATANGAS

ARCHITECT NOEL M. SARATAN

Left The house is "vernacular Filipino modern" in form, its most distinctive feature being a dominant roof with extra wide eaves. Below the threshold, the steel suspension footbridge is an aesthetic element that conceptually ties the house to the natural site.

Above Entry to the rest house is from the traditional *silong* or Filipino ground floor under the main house, amid multiple white columns. There architect Saratan's modernist wooden grill surrounds the open staircase ascending to the *sala*.

Calatagan, with its rambling cattle ranches and its famous mango orchards, nestles at the tip of the Batangas Peninsula. These rolling lands have long been private havens for the stylish rest houses of the scions of the old Spanish-Filipino Zobel family.

When Patsy Zobel first pointed out to her architect, Noel Saratan, the rugged spot where she wanted to build a modest rest house, he was entranced by the windy site and the opportunity to crown the property with a gem of modern architecture in harmony with the land. Immediately, the image of a house on *stilts* came to mind, "an elevated house to show what is going on *beyond*: a beautiful little cove surrounded by mangrove forest, a sea of tranquility tucked on the fringes of Pagapas Bay." It was a natural and inspired take-off point.

"The only thing Ms Zobel required of me," recounts Saratan, "aside from a modest three-bedroom unit, was alignment with the view and the sun's path. She wanted

to see the sea, the forest, and the sunrise and sunset on either side." Saratan's design thus takes full advantage of spectacular views of the sea, mountains, and sky, and the landlocked valley on the opposite side. To capitalize on the breathtaking seascape, the architect raised the house on one-story-high "stilts" from its perch atop a sprawling plateau: twenty concrete columns clad with the white limestone rock of Calatagan. The main house thus "floats" above ground level, providing a "frame" for the little cove below! Capturing the natural environs within his architectural design, Saratan baptized the rest house "Munting Looc" or Little Cove.

The architect opted for formal symmetry in his design. "In architecture you try to find a sense of order from what the *site* tells you. The configuration was determined to be one of formal symmetry. The plan is in the shape of a cross. On its latitudinal axis is the house itself, to take advantage of the views. On its longitudinal axis are the complementary elements: the formal garden terrace to the east (sunrise) and the hanging bridge to the west (sunset)."

The house is "vernacular Filipino modern" in style, exuding a linear horizontality within a crisp silhouette. Its most distinctive feature is its roof, which is formed of a succession of three high-pitched structures in flat brown tiles—like *salakots* (native hats)—with extra wide eaves. The wooden house below "floats" on a double (separated) beam above white limestone columns. Under the dominant roof are sliding glass panels, which allow light and wind to enter and also provide transparency! The house has the feel of a modernist *bahay*, but one still clad in vernacular materials. As Saratan says, "Wrightian linearity is very evident; it's an attempt to combine modernism and tradition."

Above The site of the vernacular Filipino modern rest house is perfect: the house faces a seaside sunrise on the east and a land-based sunset on the west.

Right A formal lawn terrace on the east side of the *lanai* is foreground for the landscape beyond: a beautiful little cove surrounded by mangrove forest on the fringes of Pagapas Bay. The architect named the house "Munting Looc" or Little Cove.

Above right The architect raised the structure on one-story "stilts" so that the main house "floats" on a double (separated) beam above white limestone columns. At ground level, the open-air *lanai* serves as a "frame" for the natural view in the distance.

Above The *sala* is clad in rustic materials: *runo* grass and mahogany wood rafters on the high-pitched ceiling and panels of *capiz* shell on the sides. The furnishing is by Yola Johnson. The photo montage is by Jaime Zobel de Ayala, Patsy's father.

Right A guest room features white cotton covers on bedsteads with bamboo details. Rustic *runo* ceilings are complemented with *buntal* (anahaw palm) shades that mute the sunlight. Room corners open to views of the rolling landscape.

The Zobel rest house is approached across a modern sandstone-tiled bridge over a two-level cascading pond and down a natural limestone driveway. Ahead, the elevated house looms high against the skyline. A formal lawn terrace on the eastward side of the ground-level *lanai* leads one down to a view of Little Cove. Westward, below the threshold, a spectacular steel suspension footbridge connecting to the next hillock conceptually ties the house to the site.

The entrance to the actual house is a modernist wooden grill arrayed around a staircase ascending to the main living/dining area, reminiscent of the stairway entry to old Filipino *bahays*. The steps rise to the *sala* under a pyramidal six-meter-high apex, a place for relaxation with untrammeled views on all sides. Saratan explains: "The rest house is actually conceived as a giant porch, exposed on both sides to capture the breezes and the views of the morning and evening sun. The wide-open living room is the simplest space in the house, comprising just the basic geometry of post and lintel, with glass panels that slide away. Wide roof eaves give protection from the rain and sun while framing beautiful views of the landscape." The master

Left Rustic materials are handled with finesse and style throughout the house: *capiz* shell panels, *tangile* wood posts and railings, and *runo* ceilings. Beyond the *sala*, the cantilevered master bedroom is supported by columns clad in limestone rocks.

Below The front elevation of the Zobel rest house reveals its formal symmetry, its distinctive "native hat"-like high-pitched roofs, and its one-story-high stilts.

Above The main volume of the rest house is like a wide, open porch with wooden slat railings on either side, deep slanted eaves under the roof, and giant glass panels that slide away—allowing the Calatagan winds to flow through.

Right The romantic master suite, designed by Yola Johnson, includes a four-poster bed, a *butaka* or traditional lounging chair, and a Chinese-style *aparador* or wardrobe. Fine woven fabrics of *buntal* palm and abaca vine dress the room under the slanted eaves.

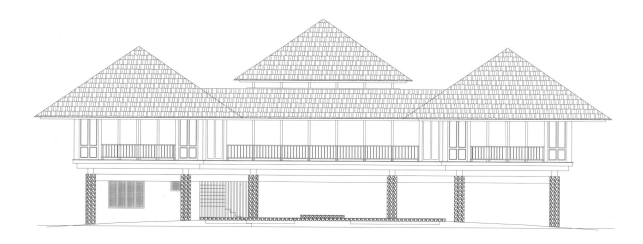

bedroom occupies one end of the house and two guest rooms the other, their corners open to views of the rolling landscape.

"The look of the house was an attempt to combine modernism and tradition. Wrightian linearity is there, but it is the more than two-meter roof overhang throughout that plays the dominant role—the traditional Asian roof overhang is clad with the natural textures of *runo* grass and wood, underlined by very linear columns and balustrades."

There is a special spirit within this extraordinary floating house made of ordinary materials which does indeed make it "restful, peaceful, contemplative, and meditative." As a fellow modernist put it: "The architecture and site planning of this house speaks remarkably well of Saratan's sensitivity and affinity to the site, and his clear understanding of how masses can be composed to articulate a design idiom for the tropics. His creative eye interplays horizontal and vertical lines into an arresting architectural whole."

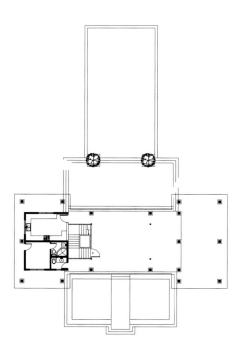

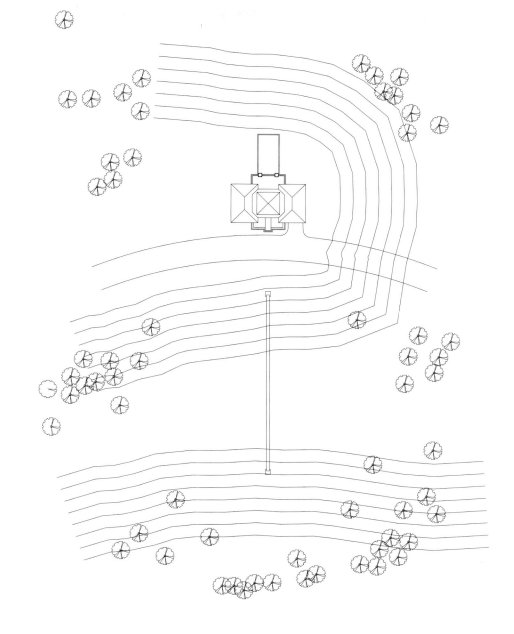

Opposite above This modern *bahay* on stilts exudes a linear horizontality within a crisp silhouette. Its distinctive feature is the roof: three high-pitched structures covered in flat brown tiles resembling *salakots* (native hats).

Opposite below The ground floor plan is in the shape of a cross on which the house is imposed latitudinally to take advantage of the surrounding views.

Above The site plan shows the formal garden terrace to the east, facing the sea, and the hanging bridge to the west.

Left The rest house is approached across a modern sandstone-tiled bridge over a two-level cascading water garden. The twenty concrete columns lining the *lanai* are clad with the bleached limestone rock typical of Calatagan.

zobel hacienda

"The rest house has a Zen-like feel amid principles of Asian Modern design: pared-down geometry, mostly rectilinear, and cubist in bent ... using stone, glass, concrete, and water surfaces, interfaced with one another, to achieve planar interplay. Clean right angles on massings in clear glass and rusticated masonry ... achieve an elegant restraint well carried over into the geometry of the modern vernacular roof." ED LEDESMA

Visitors to the weekend home of Fernando and Catherine Zobel on the rambling family estate in Calatagan, Batangas, describe it as elegant, serene, and Zen-like— "like a temple on a field." The house is built in the form of a series of modern pavilions with a distinctive profile reminiscent of an old Japanese temple. The dark slate roof, with its three points and iconic crossed rafters and finials, is the home's crowning glory.

Owner Fernando Zobel calls his family rest house "Bahay Salakot" after the native farmer's conical hat, but this is too humble a name for this awesome Aman-like "temple," which houses both a treasury of ethnic Asian

Fernando & Catherine Zobel

CALATAGAN, BATANGAS

ARCHITECTS ED LEDESMA & ANDY LOCSIN
LEANDRO V. LOCSIN PARTNERS, ARCHITECTS

Above The rest house alludes to a Japanese temple in the fields of Calatagan, Batangas. The sleek vernacular roof, with crossed rafters, crowns a ritual entry pavilion raised on a horizontal pyramid of steps and guarded by two terracotta horses.

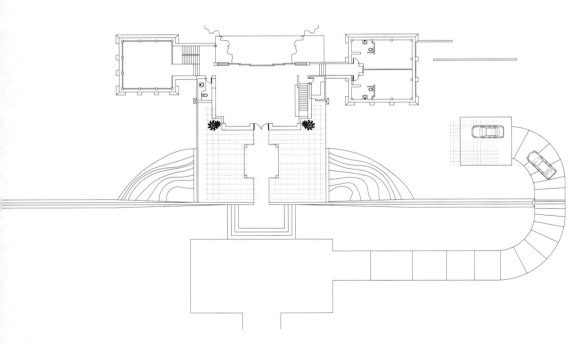

Above The dramatic approach on a country road lined with bougain-villea. The rest house first appears amid a horizontal plane of adobe wall and bamboo grove. Entry is under this formal Zen-like, wood-raftered pavilion.

Left Ground floor plan of the Zobel pavilion house.

Opposite above Longitudinal section (top) through the living/dining area and front elevation (below) of the house.

Right A unique water feature heralds the front entry: the open-air portico supported by four columns is surrounded by a shallow waterbed filled with river stones. By night, this watery plane reflects the house walls and interior lights on its surface.

art and an abundance of modernist design ideas. The house embodies the much-vaunted Asian Modern look of the Leandro V. Locsin firm: a sleek vernacular roofline, a rectilinear living space, and serene pavilions formed by planes of stone, glass, and water. The weekend home was lovingly designed by Locsin's managing partner, Ed Ledesma, whose passion for architecture is almost equaled by that of his client: "The house has a Zen-like feel and an elegant restraint in its geometry, though some may call it severe."

The rest house demonstrates the Locsin parameters of grace and beauty—proportion, scale, symmetry, and repetition—starting with a dramatic approach within the Zobel estate. Driving along the sandy road, one first discerns the *bahay* with its pointed rooftops subtly peeking over a thick grove of bamboo. Closer up, "Bahay Salakot," located on a rise, displays its vast horizontal orientation amid a landscape of rolling grasslands, seamless skies, and, in summer, bright bougainvillea hedges.

The main entrance to the house, reached directly from the road up a pyramidal flight of steps, comprises an interesting architectural water feature: a four-columned open pavilion guarded by two terracotta horses, surrounded by a shallow pool textured with gray river stones. This wide, horizontal plane of water at the entrance blends beautifully with the vertical white walls of the façade, which are in turn softened by corner windows. Natural light floods the interior during the day, while at night, lights from the house reflect on the waters outside.

Once past the wooden doorway and the "spirit wall" behind it, decorated with a carving in the form of an abstract wooden wheel, a large central area with a soaring "native" roof composed of wood rafters and planks houses the grand living and dining areas. In contrast to the cool, planar exterior, the ambience of the interior is warm and tropical, achieved by a palette of earthy oranges and sunny yellows and a fine collection of ethnic Philippine, Indian, and Thai art and artifacts, put together by the Zobels' interior designer, Johnny Ramirez.

Left Under the high-pitched rusticated ceiling, designer Johnny Ramirez has chosen a warm, sunny palette for the décor. Furniture by Budji Layug blends with the Zobels' collection of Thai and Indian artifacts and Philippine fine art.

Above The dining area is accented with Philippine wood carvings, inlaid furniture, and an abaca-textured mural by L. Carating. The stunning pierced marble panel from India, framed in concrete, screens a staircase leading down to the basement.

Right Side pavilions off the great room contain family bedrooms. The golden corridor features a dark tribal figure from the Cordillera, a photographic composite of shells by Jaime Zobel de Ayala, and an elegant Japanese temple finial.

Left The back patio demonstrates the house's restrained cubist geometry under an elegant ash-shingled pitched roof, one of the hallmarks of the Locsin firm's vaunted Asian Modern style.

Below A seven-meter proscenium without edges offers a panoramic view from the *lanai*. The lawn rolls onward to the promontory, then tumbles down to a small cove with a sandy beach.

Above right A cluster of rain trees reflect in the indigo waters of the swimming pool under with the sunset skies of Calatagan.

Below right The architectural water feature at the entry to the house provides a reflective surface for the interplay of planes and materials. This tranquil meeting of stone, concrete, portico, and pavilion then merges with the splendid gardens beyond.

Leading off the grand *sala* are two side pavilions, which contain compact bedrooms, all well appointed with four-poster beds and decorated in exotic Asian themes. The home's service areas, including a large kitchen, a casual eating area, two guest rooms, and a rumpus room for the children, are located in the spacious basement level, accessed by a flight of stairs hidden behind a wall inset with a magnificent pierced marble panel from India.

At the back of the spacious living/dining area, the house opens up, completely and magically, to a broad *lanai* framed by a seven-meter-wide opening, which allows magnificent views of the Calatagan landscape. An expansive lawn, dotted with majestic rain trees, rolls eastward toward the sunrise. At the far end of the lawn, a deep blue swimming pool shimmers between the sky and the distant sea. Beyond the Asian Modern poolside gazebo, the lawn rolls onward to a promontory garden, then tumbles down to a small cove with a sandy beach.

From the Calatagan promontory looking back at the Zobels' pavilion residence, the formal architecture of the restrained and elegant house harmonizes perfectly with the grandeur of its setting. Clearly, the architects have fulfilled the Locsin firm's ideals of proportion, scale, symmetry, and repetition. But they have also combined these with a sense of drama—in the approach to the house, in the focal entry point and, above all, in the modern vernacular roof.

wright redux

"This residential project combines Italian house planning principles, American 'less is more' practicality, Japanese modular design discipline, and Filipino notions of comfort and ease." JOSEPH ADG JÀVIER

In recent years, various architectural styles have evolved on the spacious lots gracing the sloping streets of Quezon City. In this eye-catching house, the large lot has allowed the architect the opportunity to introduce a number of different design ideas, as well as provided ample parking space for cars and for the planting of a stand of eucalyptus trees. The clients' brief to their architect, Joseph Jàvier, was that they wanted an "intelligent, naturally lighted home" inspired by an eclectic mix of influences: Philippe Starck and Richard Meier furniture, prewar Malate Art Deco houses, and Vietnamese retro colonial furniture. They also aspired to a "modern sophisticated look and the international feel of airports."

LOYOLA GRAND VILLAS, MARIKINA, METRO MANILA

ARCHITECT JOSEPH ADG JÀVIER

Above The Retro residence has distinct Frank Lloyd Wright Prairie-style under-tones, with a floating ground plane, multi-layered roofs, and a white and beige palette. The futuristic entrance pavilion and airplane wing allude to the owner's air cargo business.

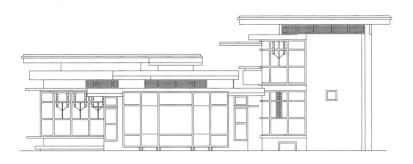

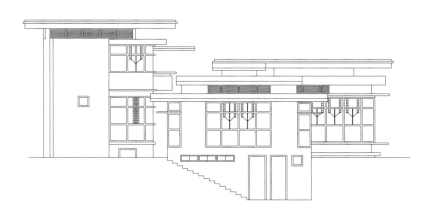

Above A Wright-like doorway under multilayered roofs opens to a dry courtyard. The house's main components are arrayed rationally around this open space, displaying strong Roman influence.

Opposite A gunmetal techno modern arcade paved in granite leads to the stainless steel door at the front entrance. The trellis, traditionally made of wood, is here composed of welded metal.

Left The front (top) and rear (bottom) elevations clearly reveal the flat multilayered roofs.

The architect obliged by designing a modern Art Deco-inspired residence complete with courtyard geometry. The house fulfills many eclectic notions, while paying decorative homage to Frank Lloyd Wright. "The idea originally was to design the house in the postwar Manila Art Deco revival style using techno modern language," says young architect Joseph AdG Jàvier. "That idea evolved dynamically as we went into construction, with the home owners in the role of project managers. The couple's preferences came through in their individual decisions, with the final product coming together as a hybrid of Italian, American, Japanese, and Filipino styles with a modern Art Deco articulation."

The house is, in effect, a retro modern take on the suburban bungalow with distinctive Frank Lloyd Wright Prairie-style overtones. The main horizontal lines are articulated with Wright's distinctive multilayered roofs and extended water funnels complemented by wraparound top-hung glazing, while the exterior surfaces, constructed of a variety of materials, are in a white and beige palette. The façade includes a mix of wood fascias, sandstone tiles, stainless steel doors, white PVC window frames, and frosted glass walls.

From the gunmetal techno modern fence, which follows the slope and bend of the road, a futuristic entrance pavilion and trellised arcade (the usual wood details translated here into welded steel) lead to the front door, where a quirky folly—an airplane wing—is suspended, alluding to the owner's air cargo business. The stainless steel door opens into a glass and granite-lined *sala*, a well-lighted but neutral space. Sunlight streams in through frosted glass walls, reflecting on polished white floors. Doors slide away within sandstone-tiled walls. Jàvier notes: "The main strategy was to provide a sequential experience. The combination of suspense and surprise is used repeatedly by the modification of the volumes and masses, the contrast between wood and glass, stone and steel. Consideration was also given to the couple's signature furniture pieces. The interiors should not compete—but rather highlight the furniture and the art inside." The home thus takes its distinctive character from a collection of retro modern furniture, ranging from Philippe Starck chairs to Claude Tayag cabinets to a Vietnamese colonial *sala* set.

In line with the traditional courtyard house, the main components are arrayed around an open, central space. Jàvier mentions "the strong Roman (Italian) influence on the space planning.... The Domus, a popular house form during the height of the Roman age, was used as a pattern for the placement of the spaces. It is practical, because it brings the outside in, and vice versa." The courtyard was originally meant to hold a large *koi* pond with a bridge for crossovers from one component to another. The idea of the pond was dropped, however, on the grounds that it would be too difficult to maintain, and the green stones of the courtyard were rearranged instead in the form of a mini plaza.

Only from the steeply sloping road does one see that part of the house is built below ground. A large arched glass panel frames a wooden staircase that zigzags down three levels to the children's bedrooms. This exposition glass window design—homage to Wright and Louis Sullivan—took three months to make. Jàvier explains: "My main design influences are Frank Lloyd Wright, Shin Takamatsu, I. M. Pei, Richard Rogers, Norman Foster, Renzo Piano, and Leandro Locsin." He also believes strongly in working within the philosophy of David Childs, one of the senior partners of Skidmore, Owings, and Merill: "Beauty is a piece of work that can hoist you in a prolonged suspension of disbelief."

Opposite above Glass doors slide away within sandstone-tiled walls, leaving a bright open passage between the granite-lined dining and living rooms.

Opposite below Longitudinal section of the Retro residence.

Above Sunlight streams in through frosted glass walls in this "intelligent, naturally lighted home." Retro modern furniture, including a Vietnamese *sala* set from Firma and a Chinese moongate display case by Claude Tayag, emphasize the home's Art Deco inspirations.

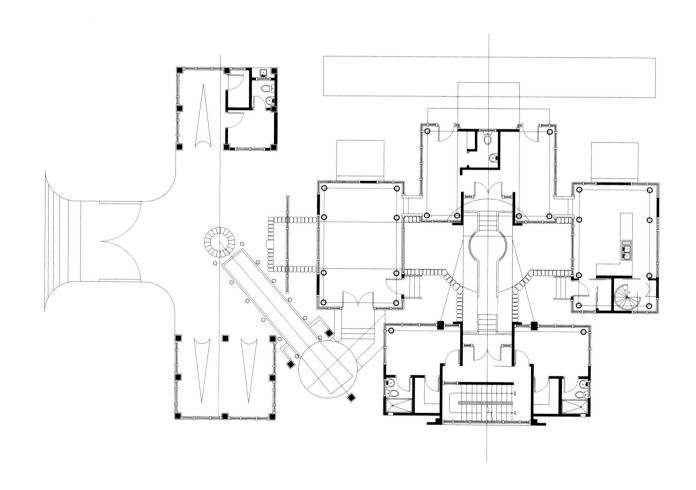

Far left This modern white bathroom features a double basin on a floating plank console. The smooth, rounded column extends from ground level.

Center Paying homage to Wright, architect Javier "floats" the house over the ground and clads the façade with a mix of sandstone tiles, frosted glass walls, white PVC window frames, and wood fascias.

Left Also adapted from Wright's Prairie-style designs are these modern water funnels extended off the layered roof eaves. The drains lead to chains which guide tropical rains to the ground.

Below left Main level floor plan.

Right This bright hallway lining the dry courtyard gets its high-tech look from the white PVC window frames and frosted glass walls.

Below Reflecting the owners' eclectic taste, this wooden set outside the master bedroom dates back to colonial Vietnam.

escheresque mansion

"The house is a living organism that capitalizes on the attributes of site, context, and program to achieve a dynamic equilibrium; a constant game of drawing curiosity and providing discoveries." JORGE B. YULO

Left The four-tiered staircase is the organizing element of the house. Its design—an intriguing play of masses and voids, positives and negatives—clearly demonstrates the designer's superb control of abstract concepts and mixed materials.

Right The back of the mansion appears like a giant birdcage by the 16th hole of the Alabang Golf course. The immense construct of concrete, steel, and glass derives from a rational mathematical module by architect Jorge Yulo.

AYALA ALABANG, MUNTINLUPA, METRO MANILA

ARCHITECT JORGE B. YULO, JORGE YULO ARCHITECTS & ASSOCIATES

Ayala Alabang is a gated residential enclave whose central section is located around a golf course and a country club complex. The prime lots are those that adjoin the fairways, as residents can enjoy not only picturesque views but also greater privacy. One of the grander houses in the enclave is the multistory mansion commonly referred to as "the birdcage." For the owner, an avid golfer, the site was a dream come true: to have a front row seat at his favorite sporting arena! The new mansion by the green was designed by Jorge Yulo, a fellow golfing enthusiast.

To best capitalize on its location, the house was elevated at the front and articulated from basement to bedrooms with a modernist metal and glass grid. This mass of concrete, steel, and glass frames the Alabang Golf Course at the 16th hole, Par 3. Golfers putting nearby often gaze at the magnificent "birdcage" set high over the green. As soon as one

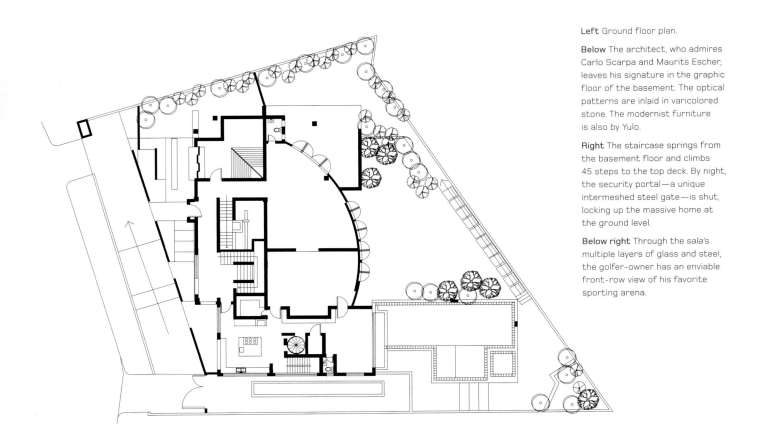

Left Ground floor plan.

Below The architect, who admires Carlo Scarpa and Maurits Escher, leaves his signature in the graphic floor of the basement. The optical patterns are inlaid in varicolored stone. The modernist furniture is also by Yulo.

Right The staircase springs from the basement floor and climbs 45 steps to the top deck. By night, the security portal—a unique intermeshed steel gate—is shut, locking up the massive home at the ground level.

Below right Through the *sala*'s multiple layers of glass and steel, the golfer-owner has an enviable front-row view of his favorite sporting arena.

enters the house from the street side, one is greeted by dramatic views of the 16th hole and the surrounding fairways through the multiple layers of glass and steel.

On the street side, the house looks quite different but is equally impressive. Architect Yulo had the site, which formerly sloped down toward the road, reconfigured, raising the front entry about one story above street level. Soaring upward some four stories, the grand modernist façade is composed of solid planes of concrete, stone, and metal. A short, steep driveway leads to the front portico, softening the lines of the imposing structure.

No windows face the street. Instead, a few openings in the multiple solid planes demonstrate a new way of articulating light and privacy. Says Yulo: "The placement of walls in the street-facing façade seems arbitrary or short of a prevailing logic. However, each solid element is correspondingly aligned with a front-facing window to inhibit direct visual access from the street, while allowing much-wanted reflected natural light and ventilation to enter the house." Beyond this sculptural façade lies the great "birdcage," its inner spaces vast and deep, and well lit with full glazing on almost three sides.

Right The open-air deck at the fourth level forms a large terrace with more views of the fairways and another cantilevered bar. The flooring is natural, crazy-cut *araal* stone with a polyurethane coating. The top terrace is a laundry area by day, but an outdoor lounge with cubist ambience by night.

Left The central axis of the
mansion is this atrium-stairwell
containing a dazzling Escher-like
stairway composed of steel,
concrete, and wood. A unique
cantilevered bar extends off
a concrete step!

Just inside the front door lies the central axis and the
organizing element of the mansion: a basement-to-ceiling
atrium-stairwell containing a dazzling Escher-like stairway
composed of steel, cantilevered concrete, and wood. Comprising 45 steps, the staircase demonstrates the designer's
superb play of solids and voids and mixed materials. Of
the atrium-stairwell Yulo says: "The house is a betrayal of
human cognitive perception. The five senses are used as
tools to orchestrate space, form, and time into a total ex-
periential performance. It is a game of dualities and juxtaposition of opposites such as solid and void, dark and light,
hard and soft." To the side of the stairwell is a small eleva-
tor, installed for the use of the owner's elderly father, which
does double duty by also acting as the stiffening, stabiliz-
ing structure in the giant module.

There are more designer surprises in store in the mansion. From the entry level one can look down to the office
area over a unique terraced system of library shelves—a
fascinating Yulo creation. In the basement there is a vast
optical illusion floor design—the architect's signature—and
out by the swimming pool abstract ornamentation deco-
rates and disguises the utilitarian pump room. Every bathroom is a unique "designer space," containing a different
expression or new experimentation. Yulo is constantly
experimenting with far-out ideas and unusual materials
to create unique washbasins, counters, and closets.

Yulo has also placed cocktail bars within the structure.
Down at basement level, the magnificent staircase extends
one concrete step horizontally to form a unique bar on
a cantilevered beam! Up at the fourth level, the open-air
deck yields a large terrace with views of the fairways—
and another cantilevered bar.

Yulo's intricate design demanded two years of his time
and some 150 drawings! His attention to detail is evident
everywhere: in the metal frames for the extensive glazing,
in the pivoted door and wood-veneered partitions, and
in the architect-designed furniture. The Escher mansion
involved rigorous mathematics and extensive horizontal
continuity throughout the space. Remarks Yulo: "The
owners will discover patterns in every direction. They will
not grow easily tired of this house, and will realize and
appreciate the harmony as the module unfolds. With
familiarity through usage and discovery, they will gain a
different and more mature experience, a sense of home."

Above The dining room on the
far end of the circular main floor
looks out toward the 16th hole
green. Floor-to-ceiling glazing is
configured in standard horizontal
glass panels, facilitating any necessary replacement of panes.

Left Sloping terraced bookshelves act as a divider outside the home-office. The wooden plank in the center forms the banister. Visitors to the house can look from the entrance down to the basement over this unique shelving system specially designed by Yulo.

Right A raised-edge swimming pool complements the lines of the rear of the mansion. A series of "false" roof modules gives the elevation a traditional Asian profile, concealing what would otherwise have been a wide, imposing roof deck.

Multiple planes of concrete, stone, and metal prevent direct visual access to the inside of the mansion. A steep driveway raises the front door midway up the façade, thereby "softening" it.

Down by the poolside, the pump room bears an abstract modernist gate designed by the architect. The house involved some 150 drawings of exacting precision and proportion.

Every room and corner contains points of interest and function, such as this green glass block by artist Bobby Castillo that comprises the bathroom sink in the master suite.

luz studio home

"If the Atrium house is a peep box and the Knox house is a camera, the Luz house is like a camera aperture. As Arturo Luz is a painter who is sensitive to light, the window openings in the living/dining area and studio are carefully sized to allow just the right amount of light into the space." EDUARDO CALMA

Arturo & Tessie Luz

VALLE VERDE, PASIG, METRO MANILA

ARCHITECT EDUARDO CALMA
LOR CALMA DESIGN, INC.

Left The house's central atrium is a stunning cubist suite in ebony and ivory. Massive (two meter square) natural-textured slabs of black slate, imported from India, form a solid base for the linear white staircase visibly climbing up to the third level. The all-black armchairs are by Le Corbusier.

Above The artist's studio home is an introverted white box within a high white fence. The dominant accent on the front elevation is a modernist concrete sunshade extended over a tall threshold window—an Ed Calma hallmark.

Arturo Luz is an icon of Philippine modern art. His prolific work, which spans half a century, influences as well as flavors the cultural landscape of Metropolitan Manila and the rest of the country. City life has always been a theme in his art, and so it was only natural that he chose to build a home in the center of the metropolis he knows and loves so well. The new urban house was also an opportunity to consolidate his personal art collection as well as create bigger and better studio space. Arturo and Tessie Luz chose a smallish lot in a middle-class subdivision just off the Ortigas central business district, and commissioned the son of lifelong friend and architect Lor Calma, Eduardo (Ed) Calma, to design a modern studio home.

The house, like many of Ed Calma's modernist designs, is a great white box where the main organizing element is a large central atrium. Because of the lot's small size, the Luzs' atrium is also the main living room. The entry is a centrally located two-story passageway that takes visitors direct from the front gate through to the main *sala* space. The two-story passageway is shielded from views and the sun by a concrete sunshade placed high above. The passageway also functions as a perfect gallery for displaying the artist's work, such as his retrospective of white wood reliefs from the 1970s held during the house-warming.

The Luz studio home is divided into domestic space and space for the artist—both work and social. The studio is located on the west side of the house, along with the living and dining areas, public spaces which can be converted into additional gallery space when necessary. The east side contains the domestic areas: the bedrooms, service areas, and garage. This functional division is visible from the front of the house, which is split in the middle by the front door canopy, an extension of the gallery corridor inside. Above the door, the large concrete sunshade breaks up the front façade and forms a privacy screen over the glazed threshold.

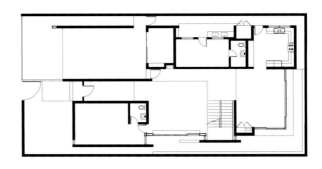

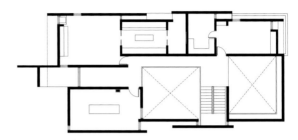

Above The ground floor (top) and second floor (bottom) plans of the Luz studio home illustrate a masterful use of a small, narrow lot to create gallery space in the expansive living and dining areas.

Left The front entrance leads to an all-white, double-height passageway which doubles as a gallery for Luz's relief art of the 1970s. Beyond the overhead bridgeway leading to the artist's studio is the soaring black and white *sala*.

Right The same black slate flooring in the *sala* is carried through to the glassed-in minimalist dining room, providing continuity and visually expanding the space. Its double-height ceiling, elevated over a fully cantilevered corner, contributes further to the open, airy ambience. A narrow L-shaped fern-and-pebble garden set next to the white perimeter wall, and the red upholstered dining chairs, introduce color to an otherwise black and white palette.

Below A bird's-eye view from the second-floor landing overlooking the central atrium. The white-railed corridor links the two bedrooms above the living room on its way to the artist's studio located across the bridgeway at the front of the house.

The atrium of the Luz house is dominated by a stunning white minimalist staircase in concrete, steel, and bleached teakwood that visibly climbs all the way to the third-level roof deck. The staircase, a piece of art in itself, was designed by home owner and National Artist Arturo Luz. Two bedrooms on the second, mezzanine level are linked by a wide, open corridor overlooking the central space, which leads to the artist's studio. Luz's tranquil and spacious studio has an unusually high four-meter ceiling. Clerestory and narrow slit windows fill the room with even light and make for muted temperatures.

Ed Calma notes: "Light is the essential element at work and play in the house.... Since the artist is sensitive to light conditions in the studio and the gallery spaces, light is carefully modulated in these spaces through the central stairwell, ceiling clerestories, and vertical slots—and from the panoramic view windows where light is diffused by the tall perimeter walls."

To the rear of the atrium is the glass-enclosed dining room, its double-height ceiling elevated over a fully cantilevered corner. To the front of the atrium, directly under the studio, is the artist's personal archive and storage. These simple, high-ceilinged spaces are all linked to an L-shaped garden that uses the perimeter wall, painted in white like the house, as a stark backdrop for a pebble bed and giant ferns that are able to thrive with little sun. The kitchen and utility areas are hidden from view and connect to the garage and maid's quarters.

On the third level, the deck, a feature which recurs in many of Ed Calma's modernist houses, expresses the same duality as the domestic and artist spaces below: a sculpture gallery is located on the west and a guest room on the east. The flat deck is most practically and artfully used as an airy terrace for evening entertainment. From here, the Luzs' guests can look out upon the old, faded, and conventional rooftops of middle-class suburban Manila.

Far left The linear staircase, designed by owner and National Artist Arturo Luz, is an architectural sculpture in concrete, steel, and bleached teakwood. The staircase reflects, even mirrors, the artist's minimalist linear paintings.

Left The narrow space between the picture windows and the outer wall contains a fern garden open to the sky. Vertical shifts between volumes created narrow slit windows for the entry of natural light.

Above The deck on the third floor was raised over the artist's studio to allow for clerestory windows under the studio's four-meter-high ceilings. The deck is also a display platform for a bronze sculpture by Luz and a terrace for entertaining at treetop level.

Below The left (top) and front elevations (bottom) of the Luz studio home clearly reveal the designer's cubist tendencies.

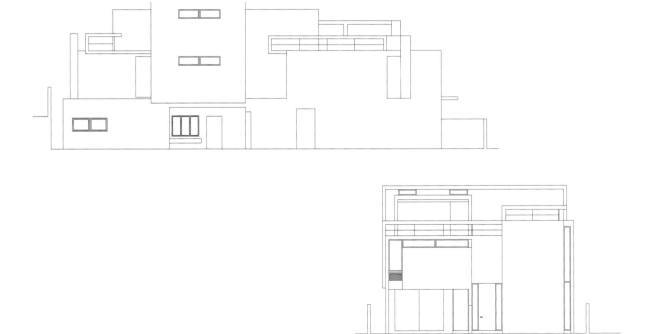

Above The simple and planar *lanai* wraps around an Oriental garden designed by Jun Obrero. A procession of slender columns leads the way to the ground-floor *sala*, set apart from the main house.

Opposite above The residence comprises several cubist volumes with a distinctly Oriental flavor: the trim and tailored ground floor is topped with Asian roof tiles and Philippine wood windows.

leviste lanai

"Architecture is an integrative journey for appreciating and understanding the human condition—one's needs, hopes, and dreams. It is a collective play of disciplines that evokes a singular statement of our time.... The Leviste architecture is a spatial composition of positive and negative spaces (enclosed and open) that coexist with one another—and express a contemplative dualism."

EMMANUEL MIÑANA

Nikki & Robbie Leviste

AYALA ALABANG, MUNTINLUPA, METRO MANILA

ARCHITECT EMMANUEL MIÑANA
EMMANUEL A. MIÑANA & ASSOCIATES

The context is suburban Ayala Alabang, south of Metropolitan Manila, élite, contemporary, and conventional. Here, among a dearth of modern white residences, the Leviste verandah house stands out. Composed of cubist volumes but with a distinctively Oriental flavor, it is noteworthy not only for its all-white masonry and clean tailored lines, but also for its dark Asian roof tiles, its shuttered window awnings propped up by *tukod* stakes, and its spatial inspirations derived from Beijing courtyard houses. Above all, it is a modern interpretation of multiple "dualities."

Home owners Nikki and Robbie Leviste, former condominium dwellers and builders, "had always liked the feeling of living in a resort!" Their architect, Emmanuel (Manny) Miñana, "had always wanted to design a resort!" A happy meeting of minds has resulted in an intriguing cluster of elevated spaces that display an overriding principle—"dualism"—the creative play and deliberate balancing of opposing ideas and spaces: positive versus negative, open versus enclosed, Zen simplicity versus Filipino familiarity.

On the surface, the Leviste house is clean-cut and simple, stripped down to smooth walls within a white fence, its modern planar form inspired by Miñana's icon, American designer Richard Neutra. What gives the façade character, however, is the injection of traditional Asian elements: sloped, layered tiled roofs arranged around a central courtyard, wood-framed windows, and slatted shutters propped up by stakes or *tukods*. "It's a simple, crisp style, quiet and cleansing," says Miñana. "The architectural approach is spiritual—designed from the interior outward, with insights dancing along the way."

Below The formal dining room, visually adjoining the open-air *lanai*-cum-foyer, is decorated in a modern Chinese style. The square wooden dining table, which seats twelve, has a broad copper inset, and was specially designed for the Levistes by Tina Periquet.

Right The two panels of an intricately carved wooden door from Rahjestan have been adapted to form a sliding screen separating the *lanai* from the cozy alcove in the kitchen where the family eats informally. On the *lanai* side, the screen is underlined by a traditional Filipino window sill or *silid*.

Left Wood predominates in the earthy yet sophisticated *sala* pavilion designed by Tina Periquet: the pitched roof of the pavilion is lined with a plank and rafter ceiling while the floor is covered with wood planks. Providing a focal point is a red bicycle painting by National Artist Arturo Luz.

The most dominant insight and another duality—cocooning versus transparency—has led the architect to create an open yet secure ambience. On the one hand, the Leviste house suggests a mysterious, introverted family home in which the occupants look toward a central courtyard. On the other, it has resort-like and "adventurous" elements. One of these is *not* having a traditional entrance or foyer. "Beyond the front gate is an open-air setting—all stilts and *lanai*!" Visitors are greeted by blue skies, Oriental gardens, clusters of bamboo, trickling water, and the dominant feature: the *lanai* or verandah.

The wide, seamless *lanai* wraps around an Oriental garden, its procession of slender columns leading the way inside and connecting to the formal *sala* pavilion, set apart like an island. The simplicity of the Leviste house is complemented by the green art of landscapist Jun Obrero—the bonsai master of their garden courtyard.

Miñana plays on positive and negative volumes, using scale to contrast volume and space, and positive versus negative space, interconnected by the "meandering and planar *lanai*." His favorite view of the house is the *lanai*. "I love the atmosphere of the *lanai* at night, when you can hear the water trickling, see the bamboo swaying in the breeze, and enjoy the private resort and garden."

The interior of the house has been made warm and familiar by interior designer Tina Periquet's use of materials

Above The entrance to the Leviste home does *not* include a traditional door to an enclosed foyer. Instead, the architect conjured up an open-yet-secure feeling to the house by a creative play between transparency (openness) and cocooning (enclosure).

Below Front (top) and r (bottom) elevations of t

Opposite Blue skies, tropical vegetation, and water features greet visitors to the house. The Oriental jar in the open "foyer" catches light spilling through the void above. Beyond this point, it is all stilts and *lanai*—the dominant design element.

and proportions reminiscent of old Chinese courtyard houses. The ceilings of the ground floor, at 3.2 meters (11 feet), are unusually high. All doors and cabinets reach up to the ceiling, their subtle lines resembling wall paneling. On one side of the *lanai*, a wooden door from Rahjestan has been adapted to form a sliding screen over the kitchen nook, a cozy seating alcove where the family eats informally. The carved screen is underlined by a *silid* or traditional window sill. Upstairs, the hallway between the bedrooms is extra wide, its sides glazed and rimmed with a suggestion of a railing to make it feel like a traditional Chinese verandah. This upper verandah looks into the courtyard below in the style of old Chinese houses.

In the evening, spotlights tucked into small white boxes focus their glowing beams on the *lanai*'s twenty-two slender white columns, exposing the austere white walls, floors, and ceilings of the resort-like home. Miñana muses on the elegant result, which merges Neutra modernism and old Beijing houses: "When the clients are flexible and forward-thinking, you can design together, dynamically! When the interior designer is sensitive and responsive to the architecture, and the landscape designer is a bonsai master who plays roughness against sophistication ... then the whole house is enhanced by the spirit of the collaborators."

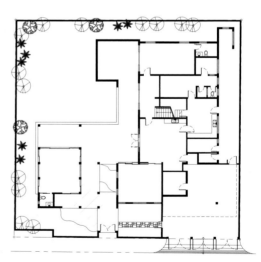

Top The informal *lanai* at the back of the house, overlooking the private courtyard, is the Leviste family's favorite spot for enjoying their resort-like residence. The wood-framed shuttered windows on the upper floor provide a warm Filipino contrast to the clean-cut, simple lines of the architecture, stripped down to smooth walls and delicate columns.

Above Ground floor plan. The separate *sala* pavilion is shown to the left of the front entrance to the house.

Right A bamboo grove by the fence is a perfect backdrop for a woven abaca lounging chaise on the crisp white-tiled *lanai*.

Above left An evening view of the house's sloping Asian-style tiled roofs over the stark and planar Western-style roof structure, here filled with dark pebbles. Miñana created this view—alluding to old Chinese courtyard houses—for the enjoyment of the occupants looking down from upstairs.

Above right The meandering *lanai* connects the units of the house at the upper as well as lower levels. The modern flat roof meets with traditional Philippine elements, such as the mahogany-lined windows with shuttered awnings propped up by stakes.

Below Rustic green *araal* natural stone was handcut and installed to resemble a woven basket on the water feature outside the *sala* pavilion. At night, the soothing sounds of water trickling down the wide wall carries throughout the Levistes' courtyard house.

Left The free-form staircase designed by Budji Layug is the organizing element and conversation piece of the house. Picture glass walls look out to the garden lining the property. The organic accent sculpture in the corner is by Renato Vidal of Binhi.

Right Giant fiberglass twine balls, given to Gonzales by a visiting European designer from Cologne, have become surrealistic installations in the stone-pebbled side setback of the house.

pasola-gonzales house

"Design is all about harmony, sensing and expressing the harmony of each object within the whole space.... I always work from a given. That given is sometimes a limitation, a restriction, an awkwardness, which is transformed into a challenge. It is a point of departure, and becomes the project's special quality." BUDJI LAYUG

Tes Pasola & Tony Gonzales

SOUTHBAY GARDENS, PARAÑAQUE, METRO MANILA

DESIGNER BUDJI LAYUG
BUDJI LAYUG+ROYAL PINEDA DESIGN ARCHITECTS

Home owners and Movement 8 members Tes Pasola and Tony Gonzales had their inspirational leader, Budji Layug, design their outré suburban home, a bungalow which shines with star quality on an odd-shaped lot. The property is only 450 square meters, but is packed with free-form design in the inimitable and ever-evolving Layug style. His creativity extends from the Mondrianesque front door to the glass "skin" of the house, to the sculptural staircase around which the house's three levels turn—in space and in spirit! At every turn there are aptly placed abstract minimalist furnishings by modernist designer-friends.

The lot, located in Parañaque in southern Manila, was an awkward trapezoidal shape, narrow up front, wider at the back, and hemmed in by neighbors on a curved road. Tony Gonzales, a graphic designer, started sketching the couple's future house himself, adding ideas contributed by creative friends. Chief designer Budji Layug eventually

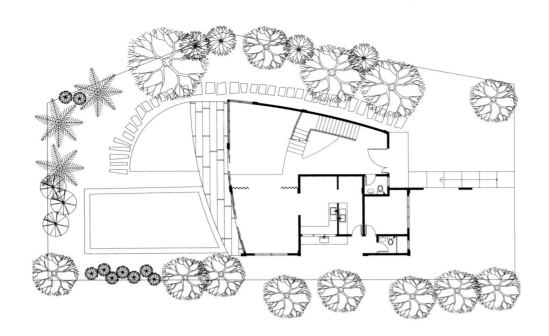

Top The ground floor plan was determined by the odd-shaped 450-square meter lot.

Below Front (left) and right side (right) elevations of the Pasola-Gonzales house.

Above left The guest room occupies the attic. Triangulated windows look down on the back yard. The furniture in natural-weave materials is by Kenneth Cobonpue of Interior Crafts, Cebu.

Above right The back yard and outer fence are visible under the staircase climbing from the foyer to the curved holding wall of the mezzanine. The *sala* contains furnishings by designer-friends.

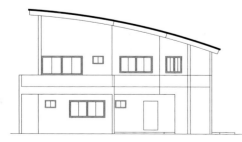

took them all on, turned their ordinary ideas upside down, and reworked the whole concept!

His new shape was an innovative geometry that defies convention. Layug says on planning a space: "I always work from a given. That given is sometimes a limitation, a restriction, an awkwardness, which is transformed into a challenge. It is a point of departure, and becomes the project's special quality." In this case, the concept was derived from the awkward lay of the land: its sloping, sunken grade and irregular shape. The Layug plan called for the house's curved outer wall to follow the curved rear perimeter

fence of the property, and for the roof to reflect the sunken curve of the land—*en air*. The result: a dominant concrete roof billowing out like a sail, echoing the shape of the land.

Gonzales smiles: "Budji really has a different eye! He grasps the space, studies it, absorbs and grapples with it, then conjures up a totally different orientation!" From ground level up, Layug abandoned the usual solutions. He moved the traditional living room to the rear, away from the street and the eyes of neighbors. He focused the activities of the house toward the back, siting a swimming pool, a spacious garden, and a private tropical view where the

sunken land used to be. Inside, he installed a grand staircase, a spiraling sculpture in golden wood and white concrete, as the creative "spine" of the house, the axis, the focusing element, and the talking point, within a soaring atrium.

For designer Gonzales, an outdoor person who loves his garden plants and jazz, Layug produced an all-glazed living/dining space, wrapping the functions of the house in a transparent skin of glass. To further extend the home, the perimeter fence was painted the same pure white as the interior walls, making the surrounding garden become visually part of the inside. Outdoors, the swimming pool reflects the trapezoidal shape of the lot.

The interior of the house is carefully planned in terms of practicality, logic, movement, and flow. The grand staircase spirals upward from the foyer area, continuing into the curved holding wall of the mezzanine. There, the family

room is a transitional, semi-private space leading off to the bedrooms and studio. On the third level, just under the roof, a small painting studio is bathed in sunlight, while a wide attic/guest room peeps down on the living/dining area and pool below.

Gonzales played project manager for the construction: "This just shows what you can do with a small space when you are not going just for effect.... The best asset here is the use of glass, which gives the house its light feeling, not just its sunny brightness, but the airiness and visual expansiveness, despite its actual compactness. Also, the radical departure from a straight-lined or two-level structure gives this a lovely extra dimension, a creative openness, expansive for the spirit perhaps? With its glass walls, the house is imbued with the necessary excitement, drama, and stimulation for artists."

Left The rear elevation reveals the concrete roof soaring over a transparent modernist space. The plan called for the house's curved outer wall to follow the curved rear fence of the lot, and for the roof to reflect the curve of the terrain—*en air*.

Below A large slate-bordered, tension-edged swimming pool follows the irregular trapezoidal shape of the lot. Though only 450 square meters in size, the property packs in a host of innovative design ideas.

Above left A cantilevered corner under the trapezoidal roof. The curved and glazed atrium wall wraps the house in a transparent "skin" of glass. At the lowest level, glass panels meet invisibly at mid-point, allowing seamless views of the landscaping and of the art pieces, effectively displayed both inside and outside the house.

Above right The front of the modern white house is all concrete planes, its dominant roof seemingly askew over the façade. The garage below rises steeply from street level over a crazy-cut stone driveway. The house is entered under the cantilevered portico at right.

hilado house

"A house—like a novel—tells a story … of the people who built it and the qualities of the place where they have chosen to build. Like a novel, a house evolves from the pragmatic to the poetic, transcending the materiality and techniques of its medium. The written words or the walls of bricks transport us to that plane wherein we can begin to understand the meaning of our existence." DOMINIC GALICIA

Alabang Hills is a gracious suburb south of Metropolitan Manila. House lots are generally less than 400 square meters and are walled in on both sides. It takes a great deal of creativity to build an interesting home on such a pedestrian site. Despite this limitation, Filipino architect Dominic Galicia has succeeded in designing a modern residence distinguished by its dynamic geometric forms, linear connectivity, and illusions of space.

The owners, bank executives Jose Emmanuel (Toto) and Lea Hilado, wanted a comfortable, warm, modern house, which made the most of the rectilinear lot. Lea's old schoolmate Galicia—who had left Manila as a journalist and returned as an architect trained at the University of Notre Dame in the United States—started by conducting in-depth interviews (so-called "couch sessions") with the couple in the belief that "architecture should be an expression of the dwellers' lifestyle and rituals; their movements should define the house."

Toto & Lea Hilado

ALABANG HILLS, MUNTINLUPA, METRO MANILA

ARCHITECT DOMINIC GALICIA
DOMINIC GALICIA ARCHITECTS

Above A vaulted skylight illuminates the interior, the line on its glass pointing north. The panel on the staircase landing is a composite of all the construction materials used in this unusual house.

Left Nine vertical wood slats hold the "suspended" buffet table, while acting as a subtle divider between the *sala* and dining area.

Right Massive top glazing and French doors comprise the circular wall of the atrium *sala*. Galicia's modernist "light-shelves" built between the levels further modulate the entry of light. The rigorous detailing was carried out by Himart Builders Inc.

Below The ground floor plan shows the juxtaposition of geometric forms on the rectangular lot.

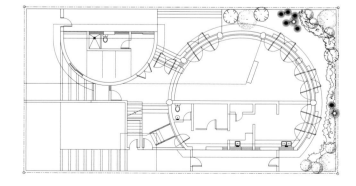

Several months later, Galicia presented sketches for a modern sculptural mass of circular volumes unified by rectilinear forms. The Hilados, taking a "leap of faith," joined him—and later the interior designer, Tina Periquet—on a collaborative journey as the house evolved from the pragmatic to the poetic. Optimizing the limitations of the site, the architect adopted three different volumes—a giant circle, a half circle, and a rectangle—and juxtaposed these in an elongated triangular formation which maximized both space and light. The resulting house, clad in brick, wood, concrete, and glass, exemplifies a vigorous play of volumes and a wide mix of materials.

It also juggles natural and artificial lighting and blends details reminiscent of Frank Lloyd Wright and the Arts and Crafts Movement, a particular favorite of the architect. As noted by Galicia: "The curvilinear house on a rectilinear lot plays on perception of space. Brick and glass produce an illusion of depth."

From the outset, the Hilado house stood in marked contrast to its neighbors. A great rustic cylinder of fine terracotta brick, made by master potter Ugu Bigyan, houses the rounded master bedroom above and the den below. The cylinder is contrasted with an adjacent white rectangular mass—the open garage—crowned by a vaulted

concrete roof with a half-moon frosted glass window which allows light to flood into the couple's spa-like bathroom. The front entry is located between the cylinder and the rectangle. Connecting and unifying the shapes is a procession of rustic wood steps, polished window frames, and intricate timber details.

Inside the house, architect Galicia has experimented with intersecting volumes and functional rooms, eschewing conventional walls and spaces—a move which defines the essence of modernist sensibility—and exploiting transparency, continuity, and a sense of "borrowed space." The Hilado house is essentially a double-height atrium house with a crosswalk over the foyer and inner courtyard, which looks down on the main entertaining area, and continues as a mezzanine hall linking the bedrooms. The rounded, glazed living/dining space "extends" outdoors to a small brick-lined courtyard outside the den, much like a mini plaza with a water wall.

Sunlight animates the living/dining area, entering through wraparound glazing, vaulted circular skylights, and Galicia's special "light shelves" under clerestory windows. In corners and junctures, natural light enters through vertical wall slits and is reflected upon all-white surfaces, lessening

the use of electricity during the day. All of the spaces flow seamlessly into each other, sharing the same air, light, and views of the garden and sky. The sense of "borrowed space" creates the impression that each room is larger than it really is. Overall, the Hilado house, with its distinctive retro look outside and its dynamic geometries inside, was a challenging architectural exercise in shaping a modernist space. However, the ordering of the functional spaces meets the owners' needs, while also making the house an interesting piece of architecture, a talking point, and a sensory delight of very mixed materials.

Through a close collaboration between the clients, architect, and interior designer, the house became "a spiritual approach to architecture." Galicia believes that every project develops a life of its own, that there evolves "grace and meaning to a house as the plan moves from the pragmatic to the poetic," and that mixing a variety of materials brings out the distinct character of each: "The materials have a discussion between themselves and we must allow that to flow!" Arnel Periquet concurs with the architect: "Every project is an opportunity for innovative approaches, new investigation ... all done with a passionate dedication to exploration."

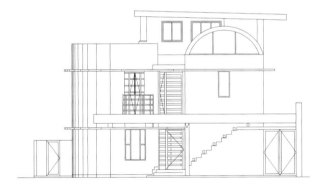

Opposite A series of skylights illuminates the transition space at the top of the stairs. Fine craftsmanship employing a variety of materials—wood, brick, concrete, glass, and metal—is apparent throughout the house.

Above left The staircase comprises rustic brick from Ugu Bigyan, white marble chip steps, metal railings, and clever lighting. The square peepholes are design elements on the outside, but by night provide soft lights leading up the stairs!

Above center A half-moon shaped soffit denotes the children's bedroom door. A tiny rope light fitted along the edge of the raised ceiling provides a soft glow by night, and safe passage from the parents' circular suite at the end of the corridor.

Above right Natural sunlight filters in over the kitchen area at the slit juncture of curved inner walls and vertical outer walls. The light reflects on the ample all-white surfaces, alleviating the need for electric lights through most of the day.

Left The front (top) and right side (bottom) elevations illustrate the geometric forms and linear connectivity which are dominant features of the house.

Left The geometry of this modern Chinese compound house is apparent from this elevated view. The complex of glass-lined pavilions is interlinked and "floating" upon a series of water pools within a courtyard landscape.

Right A 15-meter-long lap pool, built right to the edge of the open corridor, is aligned behind the "spirit wall" in the foyer. The waters of the pool thus flow toward the central core of the house, which is highly favorable for *fengshui*.

cheng residence

"*Fengshui*, the Chinese art of balancing wind and water, is defining many modern homes in the Philippines. The layout of this house is an exploration of the power and efficiency of a three-part plan: a layered wall, a floating ground plane, and a three-dimensional circulation core."

ANDY LOCSIN

Stephen & Maria Teresa Cheng

FORBES PARK, MAKATI CITY, METRO MANILA

ARCHITECTS RAUL LOCSIN & ANDY LOCSIN
LEANDRO V. LOCSIN PARTNERS, ARCHITECTS

Times and trends are changing the house geometries of Forbes Park, an established and exclusive gated community in a Manila suburb. *Fengshui*, literally "wind and water," the ancient Chinese system of designing buildings (and positioning objects inside buildings) to insure a favorable flow of energy, is influencing the architectural design of many new homes. In the 1970s and 1980s, leading Filipino architects set the tone for grand residences in Forbes and elsewhere by merging styles taken from Intramuros (the Walled City), Filipino-Spanish Mediterranean, and colonial Philippine tropical baroque. Today, a new generation of designers favors a cleaner, sleeker vernacular, a modern pan-Asian approach to the upscale Filipino home.

One such designer is Andy Locsin, who brought back from his studies in the United States Japanese-leaning inspirations from his most admired architects, Louis Khan and Tadeo Ando. His modernist eye and mindset have had a significant impact on the well-established Locsin firm's

Above The double-height foyer is the distribution "core" to all parts of the house, including the glazed bridgeway overhead. The central "spirit wall" displays an oil painting by National Artist Ang Kiukok.

Left Water plays a vital role in the residential scheme. This secondary wading pool connects squarely to the main lap pool. The bubbly zone in the foreground is a spa.

Opposite above The glass-walled far pavilion, with its high-pitched raftered roof, is the family's informal *lanai*. Family and friends gather here to make music on the baby grand or simply to relax on furniture by Budji Layug.

new era look, popularly touted as "Asian Modern." Andy Locsin's first Asian Modern residence, designed in 1998 for Fernando and Catherine Zobel, was the stunning precedent and model for nearly a dozen such homes set amid the tree-lined avenues of Forbes Park.

This new project for Chinese-Filipino businessman Stephen Cheng is both distinctively Asian and modern, with its crisp gray slate Japanese roofline, a broad, white, windowless "layered wall" at the front, and two wooden "temple posts" straddling a cantilevered entrance portico. Only the two traditional ceramic lions standing guard at the entrance and the layered Oriental roofs hint that beyond lies a modern interpretation of the traditional courtyard home, one that is laden with *fengshui* overtones.

From the street, the residence appears vast and inscrutable. Behind the layered wall, however, is a complex of glass-lined linked pavilions floating upon a series of water pools in a spacious courtyard landscape!

Beyond the layered wall, just inside the front door, a double-height foyer forms the main distribution "core" of the house. All doors, passageways, and staircases lead from here to the three pavilion components of the house. A glass-railed bridgeway traverses this foyer at the upper level, connecting two pavilions. At this point lies "perhaps the most intense architectural moment in the house: this is where a spatial link from the fronting street to the rear garden courtyard is made, opening views on either side of the bridgeway."

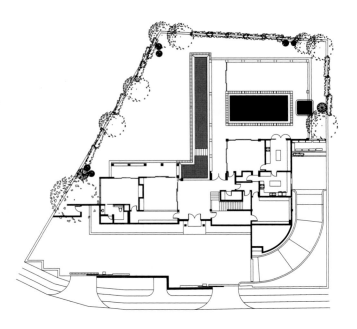

Left Ground floor plan showing the linked pavilions flanking the water pools in the courtyard.

Below By night the Cheng pavilions glow and reflect on the pond near the house. The two major water features comprise the "floating ground plane" and unify much of the home's design.

Right A mixture of tropical hardwood, tiles, stones, concrete, and water are beautifully orchestrated in the Cheng residence. The house is defined by a rhythm of wood-clad columns between masses, and framed views of other spaces within the courtyard.

In the art-filled foyer, a stark white wall hung with a colorful oil painting by Ang Kiukok represents the "spirit wall" of Chinese philosophy, a traditional building component intended to deflect evil spirits from entering a home. To its left is the smallest of three pavilions, a glass-enclosed *sala* or den, which can be converted into a guest room. On the right is the glass-paneled dining room. This two-story unit adjoins—across two connected water pools—a covered *lanai*-cum-music pavilion with a high-pitched, raftered roof. The three pavilions in the L-shaped layout embrace the central courtyard.

At ground level, the two major water features that serve both as swimming pools and for balancing *fengshui* elements unify the home's design. The 15-meter-long narrow pool aligned behind the foyer's spirit wall (its water flowing *toward* the house, down a textured stone wall, and into a well at the basement level) connects with a secondary

wading pool complete with a bubbly Jacuzzi—the "sexy water feature" requested by the matron of the household. Together, the connected pools form a kinetic water base linking the two pavilions of the main house with the third pavilion, the music room. The house's ground plane thus appears to "float" upon the wraparound waters!

The pavilions are supported by bold, square, wood-clad columns, which frame views of the adjoining pavilions and the spaces within. By night, the pavilions glow and reflect upon the waters.

The interior of the Cheng residence contains several unexpected modernist surprises. At the top of the staircase leading from the foyer is a high-ceilinged family room decorated with lounging furniture, including a bulbous bright red armchair from B&B Italia. A private third-level study nook or loft, which is reached by a steep, floating staircase made of small wooden steps protruding from the structural wall, is tucked under the soaring ceiling—a high-spirited place from where to spread *fengshui* around the Cheng household.

Above left The Chengs favor minimalist accents to create impact within the home. The dynamic white foyer (far left) displays a high-backed seat by Benji Reyes and an old Burmese temple bell. A futuristic Super Nova metallic lamp (center) is installed at the highest point of the core—by the glazed bridgeway that crosses between pavilions—and is visible from the lap pool outside. A simple Zen-like bathroom (right) with a modern-rustic feel holds a white bathtub by Philippe Starck resting on a warm hardwood floor.

Below left The front elevation (above) and a section view (below) of the Cheng residence.

Right The master bedroom is a minimalist designer suite in neutral shades of gray, complete with high-tech accessories and a muted view of the tiled roofs outside.

Below The attic, tucked under the high ceiling of the family lounge, is reached by a "floating" staircase made of planks cantilevered from the structural wall. A bulbous red armchair from B&B Italia provides a bright contrast to white and wood.

double house

"I admire the spareness and rigorous discipline of Mies van der Rohe and Le Corbusier.... This double-unit Asian-style beach house is devoid of superfluous ornamentation. It represents the fusion of a thoroughly modern architectural idiom with tropical environmental concerns." ANNA MARIA SY

PUNTA FUEGO, NASUGBU, BATANGAS

ARCHITECTS ANNA MARIA SY & JASON CHAI
C/S DESIGN CONSULTANCY

Left The designers won an American Institute of Architects Design 2004 Award for their clever use of stone, stucco, and wood in this tropical beach house. The house's double configuration comprises two Asian-style "pavilions" linked by a wooden bridgeway, a lounging patio, and a dipping pool.

Above A staircase at one end of the *sala* leads to the bedrooms and the covered bridgeway on the second level. On the left, a black door closes off the staircase to the helpers' quarters below.

Punta Fuego, a relatively new residential development on the Batangas coastline north of popular Nasugbu town, is dotted with holiday homes built in various permutations of the "Mediterranean villa," complete with tiled roofs, stucco walls, iron grilles, and decorative balconies. This holiday home, however, is different. The owners, condominium dwellers in Manila with a nine-year-old daughter, preferred privacy on their modest lot set high above a beach cove. Here they retreat on weekends to enjoy the clean air, pool, and home-cooked food rather than the sea and sand. They sought a simple, practical house, one that was turned inward. They also wanted the "feeling of a tropical resort hotel suite, with all the amenities and comforts self-contained."

When the young architects of C/S Design Consultancy suggested a *double* unit configuration—two Asian-style "pavilions" interlinked by a bridgeway and a pool—the home owners were happy to go along with the concept.

Because their budget was limited, the materials had to be kept simple, even stark. Their holiday home, which is located at some distance from the beach, has proved to be a winner. It has garnered attention in Manila's glossy magazines, made a name for designers Anna Maria Sy and Jason Chai, and won an American Institute of Architects (Connecticut) 2004 Design Award with a citation for "the use of stone, stucco and wood together.... The fact that it is in a tropical context simplified the plan. The organization of space and particularly of the volumes takes rightful advantage of the temperate climate—as the distinction between the interior and exterior is graciously ignored."

The brief to C/S Design Consultancy was quite simple: the owners wanted a two bedroom plus den holiday home for a family of three, with a large kitchen, a small pool, a garden, and ample spa space. The challenge lay in creating a sense of space and flow on a modestly sized property of 640 square meters with limited views of the sea. The result is a simple two-pavilion structure linked by a mid-rib sandstone path at the ground floor, and an open-air timber bridge at the second floor, oriented to enjoy the prevailing winds rather than the sea view.

As Sy explains, the house organization follows a diagram consisting of a "nine-square grid of sorts, with a series of interconnected open spaces visually unifying and simultaneously creating expansive views." A blue-tiled dipping pool (one watery azure square entering the austere grid) and a stone-lined lounging patio located in the center row of the house, together become the focal point of the composition—creating a cool escape in the middle of the holiday home.

On the one hand, the house is pragmatic and straightforward in terms of spatial composition, as architectural interest is achieved by the play of masses. The design concept is best observed—and enjoyed—in the linkages and relationships between spaces and functions, for example, in the open-air wooden bridgeway between the two units where one has to go outside first to enter the bedroom, and in the pool where modular stepping "stones" rise out of the water to connect the living and dining areas, thus squaring off the grid.

On the other hand, there is a sense of continuity between indoors and outdoors, as spaces blur and expand among the family rooms. The glass-paneled casually modern *sala* opens up and spills directly into the plunge pool. The outdoor dining "room" is without walls; thus the owners do poolside dinners every day. The spacious air-conditioned kitchen is as large as the *sala* itself and it

Left The family does poolside/outdoor meals every day of the week in their open-sided dining room clad with dark gray adobe bricks. The dining pavilion forms one "arm" of the U-shaped house arrayed around the dipping pool.

Above The distinction between interior and exterior spaces is ignored in the see-through *sala*, a replica of the dining area directly opposite but with the addition of sliding glass doors on three sides.

Below West elevation of the Double house. The wooden bridge-way connects two concrete masses. The dipping pool remains open to the sky, inserted into the nine-unit grid of the floor plan.

Left The spacious, air-conditioned kitchen backing the dining pavilion is the same size as both dining pavilion and *sala*! The kitchen is the husband's workshop and here his "tools" are arrayed around his Viking stove. Cooking is a congenial activity and friends gather around the large marble table to chat and chop as he cooks.

Center The double-length, mirror image, black-and-white bathroom is tucked behind the couple's bedroom wall and can be entered from either side. Adequate storage is provided by the full-length cupboards facing the long countertop.

Below A small den off the *sala*, which converts into a guest room, is smart and minimalist in appearance and function. As elsewhere in the house, matte black closets with simple handles bring clean, modern design accents to the beach lifestyle.

Right The house's divided form is clad with simple, austere materials. Rustic adobe bricks combine with off-white concrete to produce a modern Masonic feel.

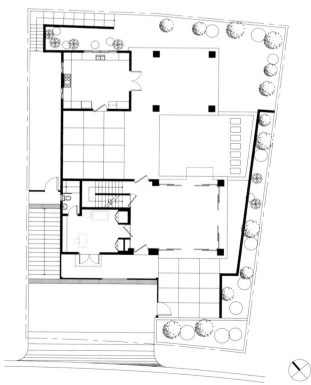

Above left The spa on the upper deck, fronting the master bedroom, offers a good home massage in an open-air environment at tree level. The owners were granted their wish for "the feeling of a tropical resort hotel suite, with all the amenities and comforts self-contained."

Left Ground floor plan.

Above The azure dipping pool— and the stone-lined lounging patio beyond it—together form the focal point of the composition, a refreshing escape in the very center of the residence.

is here that the congenial home owner indulges in his hobby, cooking, while friends and family sit around a large marble table chopping or chatting. A black "secret door" by the *sala* leads to service quarters below, where the staff have a separate living area.

The house finishes are simple, straightforward, and rigorously applied. The designers have employed contrasting building materials as eye-catching accents. Two buildings are clad in dark gray adobe bricks on the lower band and off-white concrete above. The azure pool is the visual "ornament," adding color and being an alluring "binder" for the simple gray-and-white inward-looking structure.

It is a clear, intelligent design and a comfortable living space. As the home owner says: "Architects are finding more clients who are not building houses to be receptacles of things, but rather as expressions of their lifestyle!" And as AIA Design awardee Anna Sy explains: "This double-unit Asian-style beach house is devoid of superfluous ornamentation. It represents the fusion of a thoroughly modern architectural idiom with tropical environmental concerns."

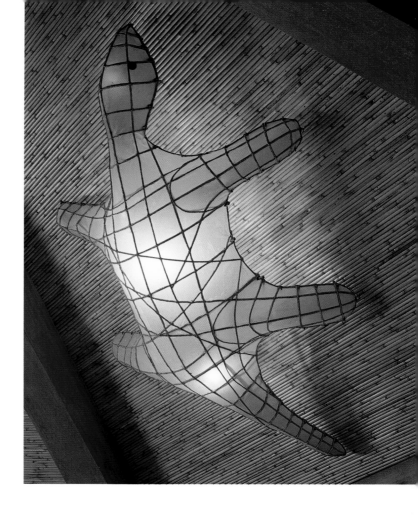

Left Six clustered octagons crown the promontory atop lush tropical gardens. Architect Mañosa used a natural palette of earth browns and beige, and integrated traditional Filipino devices to manage the climate and the social needs of the occupants.

Right Vaulted ceilings clad in *runo*, a variety of bamboo grass, introduce a warm and natural feel to the interior. This rustic treatment attracts a native gecko to the bedroom: a bamboo and paper lamp handcrafted by Wendy Regalado.

lopez pavilions

"An environmental home that is organic and Filipino.... The home owner requested an environment-responsive house that was well ventilated to catch the natural breezes of the city ... with a circular, free-flowing plan conducive to meditation and relaxation ... a home where reflection is the order of the day, with an unobstructed view of nature." FRANCISCO MAÑOSA

Great houses start with naturally splendid sites. In the 1960s, the northern suburbs of Metropolitan Manila were prime locations for golf courses serving the city's élite. Land was cheap and the courses were easily accessible from Manila's central business district. Four decades later, these rolling green sites have proven ideal for residential estates suited to up-market lifestyles.

One such landscape is the perfect site for a modern pavilion house by Francisco "Bobby" Mañosa, the foremost architect of modern vernacular projects such as the iconic Coconut Palace on Manila Bay, the Amanpulo of Palawan, and the Pearl Farm Resort of Davao. The pavilion house atop the golf course belongs to Regina Lopez, an environmentally enlightened member of one of the country's

Regina Lopez

AYALA HEIGHTS, QUEZON CITY, METRO MANILA

ARCHITECT FRANCISCO MAÑOSA
FRANCISCO MAÑOSA & PARTNERS

Below left A grand porte-cochère welcomes visitors to the Lopez octagon mansion. The edges of the porch are rimmed with a decorative pierced wood frieze that helps modulate the tropical sun.

Below right The reception pavilion, located just after the entry, is an airy living/dining terrace, open on several of its polygonal sides. The centrepiece Buddha sits surrounded by natural landscaping and a lofty view of the golf course.

Right Right side elevation of the Lopez pavilion house.

wealthiest clans. Her cluster of pavilions sits on a promontory overlooking the Capitol Hills Golf Course and the residential subdivisions of Quezon City.

Regina Lopez spoke of "wanting to live environmentally and spiritually ... wanting to be in harmony with the earth ... in a warm, woody house clad with natural and earthy materials." She informed her architect that she was "completely against a boxy, modern, marble house," favoring instead a circular, spiritual house, blessed with solar energy, an edible garden, and peaceful, meditative rooms. In response, architect Mañosa designed a nature-friendly two-story Filipino bungalow composed of linked octagonal pavilions, replete with his trademark *tukod* bracket supports under deep-eaved roofs, pointed finials over multiple roofs, and screens, scrims, and latticework to temper the tropical sun. Inside, the picturesque pavilions are clad in wood, bamboo, *runo* grass, and rattan, giving a warm, natural, Philippine ambience.

The unusual octagonal geometry informs the framework of the house's levels and spaces. Says Mañosa: "The strategy of designing a series of linked octagons enabled

us to break down the mass of the structure, and paved the way for bigger and more windows. The wide windows created the feeling of transparency and lightness, reminiscent of traditional Filipino homes. Spaces were planned with a minimum of enclosures and partitions.... Reflective of this openness, the entry pavilion is a very airy living/ dining terrace, open on several of its polygonal sides—surrounded only by the view and the natural landscaping."

The Lopez house is multileveled and multifaceted, with the main entry, covered by a Philippine porte-cochere, leading to the reception pavilion. Below this porch, the mansion terraces down the hillside some two and a half stories, almost to the edge of the golf course. The house's lush garden harmonizes with the natural slope and the existing greenery, blurring the boundaries between neighboring properties and the golf course itself. Partway down the stone path is a lawn area that forms a private garden for a guest suite tucked under the reception pavilion. The lowest level hosts a free-form *saltwater* swimming pool whose deep blue hue contrasts brilliantly with the picture postcard green of the surrounding golf greens.

Turning inward from the breezy reception *sala*, a few steps past a simple portal, the house's more private area features a living/dining space merged with a wide-open kitchen, where the owner herself likes to prepare healthy vegetarian meals for family and friends—while chatting over low-slung, custom-made kitchen counters. A staircase spirals upward to the family's private rooms which all offer splendid views of the gardens, pool, and golf course. Three clustered bedrooms each feature vaulted ceilings clad in *runo* grass and fully glazed window-walls muted with native

Opposite Three bedrooms occupy separate octagons with vaulted ceilings and wraparound windows. Spaces were planned with minimum partitions to capture the feeling of transparency characteristic of old Filipino homes.

Above The home owner's bedroom looks out over a rolling landscape. Picture glass windows are shaded with delicate rolling blinds made of native raffia matchsticks, lending a soft, muted glow to the room.

Left As Ms Lopez places a premium on her spiritual life, architect Mañosa created a personal space at the highest, most dramatic point in the house: over her bedroom. This quiet room has a panoramic view of nature.

Left The modern entry arch in the foyer functions as a traditional "spirit wall." A clay curtain of leaves made by potter Ugu Bigyan hangs from the arch's lintel. Behind the curtain, a life-size Thai Buddha image faces the front door.

Below The two-story pavilion bungalow displays Mañosa's trademark detailing: traditional *tukod* (bracket supports) under deep eaves, pointed finials on pitched roofs, and screens and latticework to temper the sun.

Bottom The ground floor plan shows the various pavilions comprising the house set among landscaped gardens.

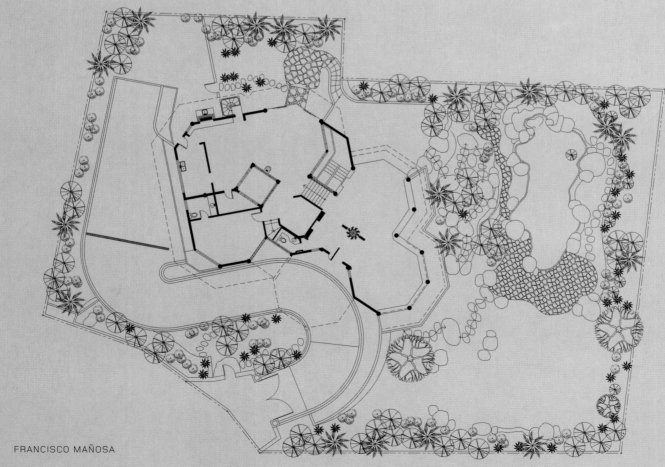

fiber shades, lending a soft, rustic glow to the sleeping quarters. Off the central television room on the second level is a sun deck surrounded by a bamboo curtain wall, and a secret garden deck with a sunken spa tub.

As Ms Lopez places a premium on her spiritual life in the octagon pavilions, Mañosa created a personal space especially for her at the highest and most dramatic point in the house: over the bedroom suite is a small but perfect meditation room with a 360-degree view. "There she can commune with nature and her own personal being ... there, where reflection becomes the order of the day, with an unobstructed view of nature."

At ground level, Mañosa has imbued a "green" life upon the house through the luxuriant tropical gardens distributed throughout the property as well as through a thematic organic "edible garden" wrapped around the wide-open kitchen. The plan includes a composting area for organic wastes, and solar power for meeting the hot water needs of the occupants.

This eco-friendly structure has harnessed the sun, earth, wind, and the natural energies of both its architect and client to become a truly splendid home.

Above The environmentally conscious household keeps an organic "edible garden" near the kitchen area. The bronze sculpture of a child held atop a hand amid the greens—"Baby Oblation"—is by National Artist Arturo Tolentino.

Below The tropical gardens of the Lopez property merge seamlessly with the wide green fields of the golf course. The lowest level of the house hosts a deep indigo saltwater swimming pool, designed for healthy dips close to nature.

martinez-miranda house

"I like understated spaces.... A controlled composition of solids and voids limits or expands the views.... It is important that our work appears rooted in its local context. This is achieved not through superfluous traditional ornamentation, but rather through a sensitive assemblage of materials and a special awareness of what is unique to the local culture and environment. We describe this as streamlined vernacular." ANNA MARIA SY

Pilar Miranda & Eduardo Martinez

DASMARIÑAS VILLAGE, MAKATI CITY,
METRO MANILA

ARCHITECTS ANNA MARIA SY & JASON CHAI
C/S DESIGN CONSULTANCY

Left A 12-meter-long reflection pool borders the dining room, located left, in the inner courtyard. *Padao*, a gaunt tribal spirit carving, stands sentinel on a pedestal, guarding the household.

Above The guest room opens onto a lush pocket garden, one story above street level. The low white fence stands atop the high perimeter wall bounding the elevated courtyard house.

Dasmariñas Village is a subdivision of Makati City in Metropolitan Manila. Beneath its polished exterior, the village sometimes faces site problems. Low elevation along the edges makes some lots vulnerable to flooding during heavy rains. Pilar Miranda and Eduardo Martinez, who have four children, sought a remedy for both the flood waters and poor ventilation. Their architects, Anna Maria Sy and Jason Chai, convinced them to raise their sights and the land itself and to completely rebuild their old house.

After demolition of the original house, the architects reoriented the new one, first raising the land by almost two meters from the level of the street and then containing the house within a high white wall that curls rounds the street corner. The new home sits at a much higher elevation than its neighbors, with the main entrance at the top of a broad flight of granite steps. The clients' brief for the 990-square meter lot included an efficient house layout, a generous garden, and pockets of landscaping. The result is a Filipino family home in a "streamlined vernacular" style.

Anna Maria Sy and Jason Chai planned a new geometry: a modern courtyard layout that is a relatively new concept among Makati residences. The plan comprises a two-story main house with two smaller pavilions at each end, one an open-sided *sala* or living room and the other a loosely attached open-air terrace or *lanai*. The reconfigured home looks inward upon a courtyard, which contains a 12-meter-long reflecting pool bordering a terrace and a lawn beyond. The living spaces are arranged concentrically around the courtyard. The children now have a central play area defined by the garden fence, as well as two pavilions whose usage will grow and change with them.

Sy explains the design: "Throughout the ground floor, a controlled composition of solids and voids limits or expands the views. Large surfaces of white plastered walls are juxtaposed against screens or doors with rectilinear patterns. Decorative ceiling rafters add texture and relief to an otherwise unadorned space. The layout, the materials, the patterns that mold this home are Asian in essence, but rendered with minimalist and modern ease."

She recalls, "It was a difficult brief, to fit a lot of functions into the house—spaces for four kids, a big kitchen, and two private work areas." To make the house multi-functional, she "borrowed" contiguous areas, letting functions merge with each other in the wide spaces. Rooms spill off the wide corridors. Floor-to-ceiling glass panels, framed in dark wood, slide into the walls to allow adjoining spaces to merge and expand with ease. The interior extends seamlessly out to the grassy courtyard and to the greenery

Opposite The family room/library adjoins the parents' bedroom, its bookcases filling an entire wall.

Right West elevation.

Below The cozy *sala* pavilion, attached to the right of the foyer, nestles under a wood rafter ceiling. Sliding glass doors open to views of the garden landscaped by Ponce Veridiano and to the open-sided pavilion on the far left.

Above The dining room connects to the reflecting pool through contiguous spaces and corridors. Traditional dark wooden frames support several layers of sliding glass doors. In the evening, artful lighting accentuates the elegance of the setting.

Below left The décor in the master bedroom is simple and understated. A work area specially for the mother is tucked behind the headboard/supporting wall—allowing her to wake up, roll over, and be in her office!

Below right White concrete walls, a dark tiled roof, and ten broad granite steps leading up to the front entrance greet visitors to the house. The lot was raised by almost two meters, and the house "retained" within a high white wall, elevated above its neighbors.

Opposite above The courtyard layout, a relatively new concept in modern Philippine homes, configures the living spaces around the lawn—including a versatile open-air *lanai* attached at the far end.

Opposite below Ground floor plan.

beyond. Small gardens placed in setbacks against the high peripheral walls serve as natural backgrounds for indoor areas, appearing like Chinese bamboo paintings.

The more traditional character of the upper floor of the house reflects the lively, interactive Filipino family who "hang out" together, especially in the ample family suite-cum-library adjacent to the parents' bedroom. Tall sliding glass doors open onto false balconies that look down on the central courtyard and the activities in the *sala*. In response to a special request, a study for the mother is tucked niftily behind the headboard/supporting wall of the master bedroom.

The Martinez-Miranda home is a simple but well-planned modern house. Sparingly detailed with flat white planes and dark wood frames, its graceful configurations and flowing spaces are particularly evident when the house is lit up at night. At present, the family is more involved with the garden and pond than with furniture and things. Eduardo Martinez describes his new lifestyle: "I was never very interested in the garden, but now it's a daily activity and personal therapy.... The garden is really a vital part of our lives and the plants are our perimeter wall!"

Says architect Anna Maria Sy, "It is important that our work appears rooted in its local context. This is achieved ... through a sensitive assemblage of materials and a special awareness of what is unique to the local culture and environment. We describe this as streamlined vernacular."

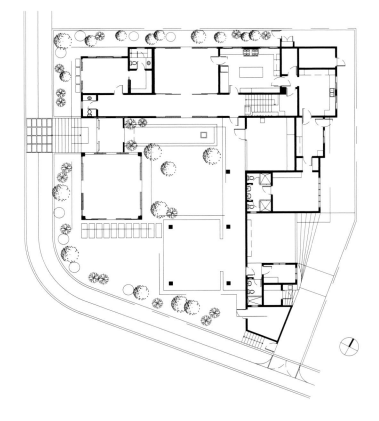

Left The Glass residence, built on a standard 450-square meter lot, stands out among houses in the old neighborhood because of its trim, rectilinear lines, its amazing glazed fence, and its matching glass-railed balconies.

Right Translucent glass filters natural light from the garage onto three pieces of art by modernist Raul Isidro. The slanted window panes are allusions to the angled screens first used by National Architect Pablo Antonio.

glass residence

"This sleek, streamlined home with a hint of both Asia and Europe—the modernity derived from Bauhaus and de Stilj of the 1930s—demonstrates my passion for integrating Eastern and Western influences in a relaxed, light home that is of today and yet timeless." RAMON ANTONIO

During the last two decades of the twentieth century, the popular "Filipino-Spanish Mediterranean" style flourished in the élite subdivisions of Metropolitan Manila. Since the turn of the century, however, many houses have been renovated or rebuilt in various versions of Philippine modernism. One architect who has successfully made the transition from the Mediterranean style to the new "Asian Modern" is Ramon Antonio, son of classic modernist Pablo Antonio Sr, National Artist for Architecture in 1976. Antonio's work is now closer to his father's original Art Deco look, but with much less use of ornate embellishment, more simplified lines, a limited palette and range of materials, and a singular use of industrial glass.

MAGALLANES VILLAGE, MAKATI CITY, METRO MANILA

ARCHITECT RAMON ANTONIO

Above From the back *lanai* looking forward, there is an easy spatial flow toward the living room under its bright atrium ceiling. Sliding glass panels bordered by dark-stained mahogany, organize the spaces and frame the rooms.

Below Front elevation (top) and longitudinal section (bottom) of the Glass residence.

Right View from a semi-enclosed library toward the enclosed dining room. The house is organized rationally, with functional rooms and social spaces linked by a wide, central corridor.

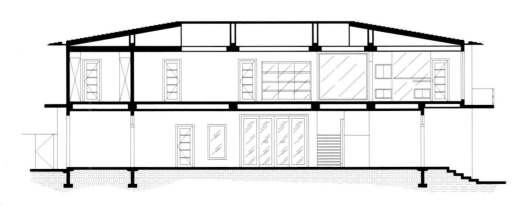

In the past few years, Ramon Antonio has established as his signature a clean, streamlined look, a fashionable new hybrid of tropical modernism, which has become much in demand. Home owners praise him for his "total styling," an attention to detail which extends to the last ashtray and *fengshui* nuance. He says, "My father's hand has been guiding me these past years ... but I am using much lighter materials and more modern presentation. Traditional Asian elements are pulled into a modern structure to create East–West fusion homes."

These principles are apparent in this compact but elegant residence. When the lawyer couple's old family house in old Magallanes Village had outlived its usefulness and become too cramped, Antonio was commissioned to start afresh on the same 450-square meter lot. The result is a compact yet spacious, relaxed, and light-suffused 600 square meters of living space that is both practical and functional. Although there is no garden to speak of on the narrow lot, a feeling of spatial openness is achieved with views of bamboo-lined perimeter gardens, a double-story atrium, and an enclosed *lanai* or patio.

The façade of the house, with its clean modernist harmony and horizontality, its expansive windows and multiple balconies, and a tiled roof silhouette that is subtly Asian, is pure new, modern, and evolved Antonio. Although Antonio has included his favorite detail—wood-shuttered windows adapted from Straits colonial architecture—what is most striking about the house is his use of stark white

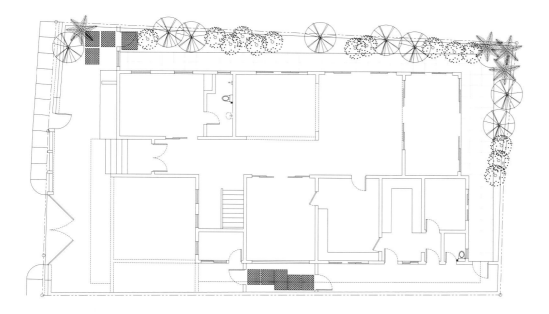

Opposite Silvered metal and reflective glass in the sleek and steamlined corridor approaching the *sala* provide a stunning contrast to the floating console tables, armchairs by Antonio, and giant mirror by Philippe Starck.

Above A clear glass railing rims the wide mezzanine corridor on the upper floor. This spacious corridor between bedrooms receives natural light from the upper level of the glazed atrium.

Left The simplicity and symmetry of the ground floor plan reflect the architect's signature stream-lined look.

concrete interspersed with wide planes of glass glazing along the street-side fence and the upper-story balconies. Industrial glass and whiteness thus combine to form Antonio's Asian Modern façade. At night, the house resembles a jewel box amid the dense locale of old residences and hoary mahogany trees in which it is set.

On entering the house, one immediately feels the expansiveness and lightness inherent in the design. The house is organized rationally on both levels, with rooms linked by a wide, central corridor. On the ground level, there is a progression of social spaces from an enclosed space (den) to a semi-enclosed space (with two sides open) to the formal main living room under a double-height ceiling. The home flows inward through multiple wood-framed sliding doors to an enclosed *lanai*, the favorite eating-cum-lounging space of the family—and of most Filipinos! Beyond the back *lanai* is a two-meter paved apron setback from the white periphery wall, a space for light and air to enter.

The "coolest" room in the Glass residence is, aptly, a pale celadon green kitchen, its walls completely glazed in green-toned translucent glass. All around the home, cantilevered and built-in wall shelves hold antique jars and books, while tribal artifacts have been mounted in the best possible places—all arranged by the "total stylist" Ramon Antonio.

Above The "coolest" room in the house, with the most innovative use of materials, is the kitchen. Its translucent celadon-toned glass walls are not only soothing to the eye but provide a hygenic environment.

Opposite above left Six acrylic paintings by artist Raul Isidro are arranged symmetrically over the floating console as part of the total styling by architect Ramon Antonio himself.

Opposite above right The staircase is simple yet artful. Every level displays a piece of art or an artifact from East or West. On the pedestal below the stairs stands an old Sung Dynasty jar from Butuan, subtly highlighted by indirect lighting.

Opposite below left The white concrete walls and the industrial glass used in the expansive windows harmonize both materially and structurally with the glazed fence and balconies and the Asian-style tiled roof in this model "Asian Modern" house.

Opposite below right The setback from the outer wall forms a two-meter-wide paved apron around the entire house. This all-white hard landscape with its own glazed gateway provides the *sala* and *lanai* with views of bamboo-lined perimeter gardens.

atelier extension

"I employed the principle of 'build it once, build it right' in the project. I wanted to create a future ancestral home ... a home that would not only be a shelter, but also enhance and develop the minds and creativity of each person that it houses." BENJI REYES

LA VISTA, QUEZON CITY, METRO MANILA

DESIGNER BENJI REYES

Left A three-level tower, fondly called "the gazebo," extends behind the main house. Made of *dungon*, a Philippine ironwood, it is crowned with a distinctly Asian roof with wide eaves. The designer used the natural three-meter drop of the land and built upward.

Above The lower terrace of the atelier tower comprises an open-air deck. This woody venue serves as a lively activities area for the family and visiting artists.

This striking combination residence/atelier is built on a steep slope overlooking the Marikina Valley, east of Metropolitan Manila. In their design, the original architects, Jose Mañosa & Associates, exploited the sharp incline to achieve maximum views of the distant mountains. The art-loving home owners then commissioned wood sculptor and furniture designer Benji Reyes to execute the design as well as to add an adjoining artists' studio. The residence thus comprises two interlinked, vertical parts: the main structure and the studio.

The main two-story house has a crisp, contemporary façade, its expansive glazing showcasing the grand staircase in the entrance foyer. Behind the main house, leading off the first level, which is raised above a basement, stands a three-level all-timber atelier of open-air terraces with a distinctly Asian roof and wide eaves. The separate structure, whose decks are devoted to the arts and leisure, resembles a wooden tower. In Reyes' words, it is a venue "for the

Left The modern *sala*, floored with exquisite Philippine *dao* hardwood recycled from an old house, is furnished with Swedish sofas from Bo Concepts. The wall mural is by abstract painter Gus Albor.

Below left The dining room, adjacent to the *sala*, is raised on a platform between square columns. At its heart stands Reyes' twelve-seater "fiesta" dining table made from a solid block of *narra* wood.

Below right The master bedroom is designed around a "floating platform" bed made from three native woods: *molave*, *kamagong*, and *tindalo*. The bed is flanked by large windows with adjustable shutters. The small watercolors above the headboard are by Fred Liongoren.

Bottom Right side elevation of the main two-story house.

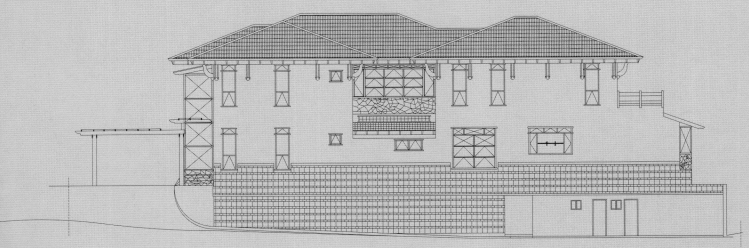

creative individuals who will live and grow here, or pass through and experience the owners' artful lifestyle."

At the front of the main house, a rustic wooden trellis-like gate and porte-cochere make a distinct contrast to the contemporary cement and glassed façade, at the same time providing an aesthetic link to the architecture and materials of the gazebo-like atelier on the slope behind.

The steep site has influenced the character of the landscaping. The back flaunts a natural look, with deep *koi* ponds and gurgling waterfalls arranged under the towering studio. Surrounding the studio is a lush tropical garden with stone paths snaking among trees and giant ferns. Nature thrives happily here, while Filipino artists thrive

on the three open decks under the wide Asian roof.

The construction of the studio as well as the interiors of both main house and atelier showcase designer Benji Reyes' facility with his chosen medium: recycled Philippine hardwoods. Collected and reworked into modern architectural details, the woods assume myriad forms and textures, from rough to polished, linear to curvilinear, ordinary to sensory-organic! The residence's main floor is a vast plane of rare, striated *dao* wood—which became available just months into the house project! In the tower, wood is used as structural framing and in screens, dividers, furniture, and accessories. The dining room is enhanced with a modernist wooden table and four wavy "woven" screens forming a

Above left The striking all-wood Asian tower of open decks and wide eaves alludes to a Balinese pavilion or a Malay house on stilts.

Left A simple wooden bridgeway connects the uppermost deck of the tower to the airy *lanai* of the main house. The lower level is a lounging area surrounded by two deep *koi* ponds and waterfalls.

Above The façade of the crisp concrete house on high ground displays expansive glazing show-casing an Art Deco staircase, generous wood-trimmed windows, and a wood trellis uniting the outer gate and the front door.

divider between the living and dining areas. The staircase comprises an Art Deco-inspired signature work by Reyes, installed over a bed of pebble stones.

The Atelier abode has been lovingly handcrafted from a treasure-trove of old materials, the result of serendipity as well as sheer good luck, that have been polished and adapted by wood-loving artisans! No set standards were followed for the height of the window sills, doors, counters, and banisters in the house. All were custom-fitted for the art-collecting owners. Wood artist Reyes says: "The house took three years to build, including collecting the recycled wood for the project. Aside from the structural plan based on the blueprints provided, the entire house down to its minute details was accomplished using my

sketches drawn on walls and hands-on discussion with the carpenters and craftsmen. I find it relevant and vital to transfer my ideas directly to the craftspeople who execute them on site. In designing this way, 'The eye is mightier than the technical pen!'"

The Atelier abode illustrates clearly the robustness of a structure that has evolved in a highly individualistic and serendipitous way! Needless to say, during the close collaboration on this two-part atelier house, the home owners and the Reyeses developed the close friendship of *compadres* (kinsfolk). The designer says: "The house has valuable lessons to teach about resource conservation, recycling, continuity and change—and raising intelligent individuals in a handmade homestead."

Ramon Antonio

Born in Manila, Ramon Antonio is a second-generation Filipino architect. His father, Pablo Antonio, was a well-known architect schooled in London who introduced the Art Deco style in Manila buildings after traveling extensively in Europe. Pablo Antonio was designated "National Artist for Architecture," the highest cultural award given by the Philippine government. After graduating with a degree in architecture from the University of Santos Tomas in Manila, Ramon literally followed in his father's footsteps by making the same grand tour of Europe. This travel experience, combined with his architectural pedigree, augured well for him and since the 1970s he has established a reputation as residential architect of choice for Manila's élite. Dozens of his houses dot Metro Manila's exclusive enclaves such as Forbes Park, Dasmariñas Village, Bel Air, and Alabang Village. Today, he continues his work in an updated genre of tropicalism mixed with the modern functionalism that his father pioneered.

Ramon Antonio

Unit 1203 "139 Corporate Center," 1339 Valero Street, Salcedo Village, Makati City, Philippines

Tel: (632) 813-7330
Fax: (632) 813-7331
E-mail: rrantonio@axti.com

Eduardo Calma

Eduardo (Ed) Calma is the son of Lor Calma, an icon of modernist Filipino design who introduced postwar Philippines to trends from the West. Ed received his BA in Architecture from the Pratt Institute in Brooklyn, New York, in 1988, and continued his education at the Pratt International Studies School in Rome before taking his MSc in Advanced Architectural Design at Columbia University, New York. He then worked for Giovanini & Associates and Ellerbe Becket, both in New York, before returning to the Philippines in 1991. Ed continues his father's mission of modernizing and minimalizing Philippine design. He has produced a notable body of work that has been published internationally, including the Josephine Knox House in Punta Fuego, Batangas; the Calma Residence in Dasmariñas Village, Makati; 12 Restaurant in Makati, and the La Vista House in Quezon City. He is currently designing a new building for the College of Design and Architecture of De la Salle University in Manila.

Lor Calma Design, Inc.

G/F State Condo, 186 Salcedo Street, Legaspi Village, Makati City, Philippines

Tel: (632) 817-8465
Fax: (632) 816-74514
E-mail: ecalma@lorcalma.com

Dominic Galicia

Although he was born and raised in Manila, Dominic Galicia moved to the United States in his teens. He did his undergraduate studies at the University of Notre Dame in Indiana and his graduate studies in architecture at the Pratt Institute in Brooklyn, New York. Galicia worked for several American architects, such as Douglas Korves, Roger Sahli, and Naomi Leff, before returning to his homeland. He has established a reputation for innovative residential design along with notable institutional work, seen in the Summit School at Fort Bonifacio in Taguig City and two chapels: the Adoration Chapel in Makati City and the Archbishop's Chapel in Intramuros, Manila.

Dominic Galicia Architects

Solid House, 2285 Pasong Tamo Extension, Makati City, Philippines

Tel: (632) 729-3277
E-mail: galicia@globelines.com.ph

Jeff F. Isidro

Godofredo (Jeff) F. Isidro, who comes from Marikina City on the western fringes of Metro Manila, earned his BSc in Architecture from the College of Architecture, University of the Philippines, and went on to do graduate studies in Landscape Architecture at the same university. In 1987, he moved to Singapore where he had stints with several top Singaporean architectural firms such as Raglan Squire and Partners. In Singapore, he was involved in several conservation projects, which won awards from the local planning authority. In 1995, Jeff returned to Manila to set up practice—The Ampersand Architects—with three former classmates. The work of the firm ranges from the design of boutiques, restaurants, and residences to housing complexes and institutional facilities. Isidro has designed and is supervising the building of one of the largest mosques on the southern Philippine island of Mindanao.

The Ampersand Architects

Unit 5 3rd Floor, Sunshine Condominium, 9633 Kamagong cor. Guijo Street, Makati City 1203, Philippines

Tel: (632) 895-0248
Fax: (632) 899-5898
E-mail: Jeffie@Qinet.net

Joseph AdG Jàvier

Joseph Alexander de Guzman Jàvier, born in Quezon City in 1973, has a Certificate in Building Technology and a BSc in Architecture from the College of Architecture, University of the Philippines. After graduating in 1995, he held positions as senior design draftsman and administrative architect with RR Payumo & Partners before joining Filinvest Alabang as architect. In both firms, he was largely responsible for the administration of various projects in different phases of design and construction. In 1996, he set up his own firm, Jàvier, in Alabang Muntinlupa City, Metro Manila. He handles the overall management of the firm, which focuses primarily on public, sacred, and hospitality projects.

Jàvier

D1 FREB Building, Santa Teresita Street, Villa Donata, Alabang, Muntinlupa City, Metro Manila Philippines

Tel/Fax: (632) 807-2605
E-mail: javierarchitects
@pldtdsl.net

Budi Layug

Antonio "Budji" Cancio Layug, born into a Filipino furniture manufacturing family in 1950, did his undergraduate studies at Ateneo de Manila and the University of Santo Tomas and graduate studies at the New York School of Interior Design. Over the last 25 years, he has established an international reputation for his designs using natural Philippine materials, and has become a successful exporter of exquisite high-end furniture. In 1999, he instigated a new design thrust in modernist furniture using natural materials with the formation of Movement 8, a select group of designers committed to raising the design image of the Philippines who exhibit at international trade shows. Known as a "complete designer," Layug's design works include the Zulueta pueblo house in Tagaytay, Alliance Française de Manille, Tagaytay Highland Country Club, Discovery Shores Boracay Resort, B Living Showroom in Bangkok, and the Trees Sathorn in Bangkok.

Budji Layug+Royal Pineda Design Architects

235 Nicanor Garcia Avenue, Bel Air III, Makati City, Philippines

Tel: (632) 896-6316
Fax: (632) 896-6348.com.ph
E-mail: budjilayug
@budjiroyal.com.ph

Ed Ledesma

Edgardo (Ed) L. Ledesma Jr has a BSc in Architecture from the University of Santo Tomas. Managing Partner of Leandro V. Locsin Partners since 1998, he is credited with the development of the firm's design sensibilities. He has been involved in many of the firm's most important projects, among them the Cultural Center of the Philippines Theater for the Performing Arts, the Hotel Intercontinental Manila, and the Istana Nurul Iman (State Palace for the Sultan of Brunei). More recently, he was Partner-In-Charge for Tower One and the Philippine Stock Exchange Plaza; Kawayan Cove in Nasugbu, Batangas; and the new Ayala Museum. Ledesma has also overseen many of the firm's residential urban and rural commissions, including those of Fernando Zobel, Menchu Katigbak, Ricardo Yanson, Inigo Zobel, Rante Aguila, and Emmanuel Sy. He is a Corporate Member of the United Architects of the Philippines, Makati chapter.

Leandro V. Locsin Partners, Architects

18th Floor, Locsin Building, 6752 Ayala cor. Makati Avenues, Makati City, Philippines

Tel: (632) 816-7927/28
Fax: (632) 817-1998
E-mail: lvlparch@pldtdsl.net

Andy Locsin

Administrator and Design Consultant to Leandro V. Locsin Partners since 1995, Leandro (Andy) V. Locsin is responsible for formulating office policy and serving as an internal critic and design consultant on various projects within the firm. He has been involved in several of the firm's high-profile projects, such as the Monastery of the Transfiguration in Malaybalay Bukidnon, NetOne Center, Kawayan Cove, the Makati Pedestrianization project, Tower One and Philippine Stock Exchange Plaza, the new Ayala Museum, and more recently, the Serendra development at Fort Bonifacio, Makati. He has brought the firm's modern vernacular "signature" to major residential projects around the country, including those of Xavier Loinaz and Jaime Augusto Zobel in Batangas; Francisco Bayot in Baguio; Menchu Katigbak, Ricardo Po, and Carlos Elizalde in Makati; Gabby Lopez in Quezon City; Dante Go in Tagaytay; and Inigo Zobel in Boracay. Andy Locsin earned a BA from Wesleyan University, Connecticut, in 1984, and a Masters of Architecture from Harvard University, Massachusetts, in 1989.

Leandro V. Locsin Partners, Architects

18th Floor, Locsin Building, 6752 Ayala cor. Makati Avenues, Makati City, Philippines

Tel: (632) 816-7927/28
Fax: (632) 817-1998
E-mail: lvlparch@pldtdsl.net

Francisco Mañosa

Francisco "Bobby" T. Mañosa earned his BSc in Architecture from the University of Santo Thomas in 1953. Since then, this vastly experienced architect has worked in several countries in Asia, Europe, and the United States and has received numerous awards for his work. He was the first recipient of the Golden Award in the Field of Filipino Architecture given by the United Architects of the Philippines in October 1989. In May 1994, he was named the Most Outstanding Professional of the Year by the Philippine Regulations Commission, and in June 1996, he received the Design Award for Excellence in Architecture from the United Architects of the Philippines. In 2004, he was selected by the Philippine Jaycee Senate & Insular Life as one of the Five Outstanding Filipino (TOFIL) Awardees in the area of Architecture. In February 2005, he was granted the Gawad Gintong Likha Award by the Architectural Archives of the Philippines (the United Architects of the Philippines & the Philippine Institute of the Philippines), and in June 2005, the University of Sto. Tomas granted him the Outstanding Thomasian Alumni Award in Architecture.

Francisco Mañosa & Partners

19th Floor, The JMT Corporate Condominium, ADB Avenue, Ortigas Center, Pasig City, Metro Manila, Philippines

Tel: (632) 633-8742/45
Fax: (632) 631-8823
E-mail: mail@manosa.com

Emmanuel Miñana

Emmanuel (Manny) Miñana is a forty something architect much sought after for his residential and hospitality design. After completing his architectural studies at the University of the Philippines, he worked for Gabriel Formoso & Partners, a leading architectural firm in Manila, known for its corporate and residential work. Miñana's notable projects include the Lakeside Leisure Country Club in Talisay, Batangas; the APEC Summit Presidential Villas in Triboa Bay, Subic, Zambales; the La Salle Christian Brother's Chapel and Memorial Cloister and Gardens, and the Baguio Country Club's Hamada Restaurant in Baguio City. Aside from residential work in Metro Manila, he has also completed residential projects in the southern provinces of Batangas, Cebu, and Davao as well as vacation villas in Indonesia, Malaysia, and Saudi Arabia.

Emmanuel A. Miñana & Associates

34 Sto. Domingo Street, Urdaneta Village, Makati City, Philippines

Tel: (632) 810-6508/817-3543
E-mail: eaminana@pacific.net.ph

Conrad Onglao

Conrad T. Onglao has a Bachelor of Architecture from the University of Santo Tomas. After graduation, he worked as a senior draftsman for the Philippine Foundation in Makati before moving to California where he spent the next thirteen years gaining architectural and design experience in a wide range of areas. Between 1979 and 1992, he worked in various positions for several Californian architectural firms, including Langdon, Wilson & Mumper Architects (primarily multistory office buildings); Lee & Skahara Associates (restaurants); Don Roser (boutiques); Concepts 4 (hotels in California); Kent Roxford (offices, restaurants, and residences in Japan); Chhada/Siembeda Partners (hotels in Japan); Harold Thompson & Associates Design Consultants (hotels in Taiwan, Korea, Australia, and Kenya), and Asian Resource Design (country clubs, condominiums, and residences in California, Japan, and Malaysia). In 1992, he returned to the Philippines to set up practice. He is currently the managing director of CT Onglao Architects (formerly known as ADR Design Associates) in Makati. The company is mainly involved in residential and corporate architecture.

CT Onglao Architects

Penthouse A, LPL Mansion, 122 LP Leviste Street, Salcedo Village, Makati City, Philippines

Tel: (632) 893-9174/5
Fax: (632) 893-9225
E-mail: ctoarchitects@pldtdsl.net

Marta Pedrosa

Marta Pedrosa was born in Manila but raised and educated in London. She obtained her BA (Hons) at the University of Westminster (1991), and Diploma in Architecture at the Bartlett School, University College London (1996). Pedrosa started her professional career with noted minimalist architect Claudio Silvestrin. Her main involvement at this stage was the design and layout of the Hombroich Project featuring the work of Tatsuo Miyajima and Robert Mapplethorpe. She also did a four-year stint with Roland Cowan Architects, working on upscale properties in London. After her breakthrough home project, which is featured in this book, Pedrosa then ventured out on her own. She has been in private practice with two London-based architects, Richard Buck and Miranda Burton, specializing in high quality modernization. She is currently in Manila working on several residential commissions.

Marta Pedrosa

Tel: (63915) 579-8270;
UK (+44) 7760131535
E-mail: martapedrosa @mac.com.ph

Royal Pineda

Royal Christopher Lopez Pineda, at 30 the youngest architect featured in this book, graduated from the Architectural College at the Polytechnic University of the Philippines before working five years for leading architectural firm Leandro V. Locsin Partners under mentor-architect Ed Ledesma. In 2001, Pineda became managing director, then architectural partner, in the Budji Layug design studio. Pineda has collaborated with Budji Layug on various high-profile commissions, such as the Roque and Lopez-Feliciano residences, the M-Café at the new Ayala Museum, and at two resorts in Thailand: Discovery Shores Boracay and the Trees Sathorn. He has also worked on other foreign-based projects, such as the B Living showrooms in Thailand and Malaysia.

Budji Layug+Royal Pineda Design Architects

235 Nicanor Garcia Avenue,
Bel Air III, Makati City, Philippines

Tel: (632) 896-6316
Fax: (632) 896-6348.com.ph
E-mail: royalpineda
@budjiroyal.com.ph

Benji Reyes

Benjamin (Benji) Lizo Reyes wears many hats: as sculptor, cabinet maker, furniture designer, and design consultant. He studied architecture at the University of Santo Tomas (1977–80) and fine arts at the University of the Philippines (1980-3). Upon graduation, Benji embarked on a vocation as a wood artist, creating individualist furniture exclusively using recycled Philippine hardwoods. Apprenticing with master cabinetmakers, he perfected a handcrafted method of bending, shaping, and fitting recycled wood into fluid-lined "functional sculptures," exquisite pieces of art that would be passed on as heirlooms. After twelve years of signature chair-making, he built his own three-pavilion wooden house in Antipolo, and the Atelier house featured in this book. Since 1991 he has held twelve solo exhibitions of Benji Reyes furniture.

Benji Reyes

16 1st Avenue, Beverly Hills Subdivision, Antipolo City, Metro Manila, Philippines

Tel/Fax: (632) 696-3809
E-mail: woodwork_breyes
@yahoo.com

Noel M. Saratan

Noel M. Saratan was born, raised, and educated on the island of Negros in the Visayan islands of the Philippines. He is from Talisay City, not far from the island's capital Bacolod, where he finished his architectural degree at the La Consolacion College. Saratan then moved to Manila to take his government exams and to apprentice with Manila architects. He worked his way up to designer in the firm of Leandro V. Locsin Partners. He left the firm in 1993 to establish his own practice. He has been a favorite architect of élite families like the Zobel de Ayalas who have built large country estates or sprawling vacation houses in the seaside province of Batangas.

Noel M. Saratan

E-mail: nc_saratan@mac.com

Anna Maria Sy

Anna Maria V. Sy was born in Manila. In 1984, she graduated BA with a Minor in Architecture from Sarah Lawrence and Barnard College, Columbia University, and in 1989 she earned a Masters in Architecture from Harvard University. After working for six years for firms like SOM in California, where she was involved in designing beachfront hotels, corporate offices, and amusement parks, she formed a partnership with classmate Jason Chai. Operating out of Connecticut in the United States and also from Manila, their design consultancy is noted for its high-end condominium work in New York City, the branches of the International Exchange Bank of the Philippines, the Net One Center at Fort Bonifacio, Kai Restaurant, and several vacation homes south of Manila. One of these homes, featured in this book, won her and Chai the American Institute of Architects (Connecticut) 2004 Design Award.

C/S Design Consultancy

7th Floor, Adamson Center,
121 Leviste Street, Salcedo Village,
Makati City, Philippines

Tel: (632) 893-0555
Fax: (632) 893-0196
E-mail: anna_s
@csarchitecture.com

Milo Vasquez

Camilo B. Vazquez, a graduate of the College of Architecture of the University of Santo Tomas, has been in private practice since 1977, working with clients both in the Philippines and abroad. He formed Vazquez & Associates, an architectural and interior design firm, in 1985 and is presently the managing partner. The firm is engaged in the design and development of various projects both in the Philippines and abroad, including hotels and resorts, retail outlets, and private residences. Vazqueuz's experience and expertise in project management and in the technical aspects of architecture have gained him a wide and loyal clientele. Local projects include Le Soleil de Boracay Hotel, Boracay, Aklan; MC New Coast Resort & Villatel Corp., Boracay, Aklan; One White Beach Resort & Spa, Boracay, Aklan; Landco/Canyon Woods, Batangas; Dencio's Bar & Grill, Alabang; Red Ribbon Bakeshop Inc.; Delifrance Coffee Shops; Studebaker's Manila, Makati; Via Mare Coffee Shops; Louie Ocampo Residence, Greenhills; Rafael Alunan Residence, Quezon City; Ambassador Lhuillier Residence, Makati; Linea Italia Group. International projects include Snoopy Place, Korea; Plaza Singapura Snoopy Place, Singapore; Pacific Gardenia Hotel, Saipan; Viamar Esplanade, Singapore; and Vietlang Chime's, Singapore.

Vazquez & Associates

27 Kanlaon Street, Quezon City, Metro Manila, Philippines

Tel: (632) 731-7356
E-mail: vazland@skyinet.net

Jorge B. Yulo

Jorge Manuel B. Yulo was born in Manila but moved to the United States in his early teens. He finished college at Simon's Rock of Bard College and took graduate studies at the Renselear Polytechnic University and the Asian Institute of Management. He worked for Cabrera/Barricklo & Associates in the United States and with Leandro V. Locsin Partners when he returned to the Philippines in the 1980s. Yulo's portfolio of notable works includes the Lupton House in Tagaytay City, the Gonzalez House in Los Baños, the Cibo and Café Bola restaurants, and the Ark Church in Santa Rosa, Laguna province, south of Manila. He is currently working on several large residential projects in and around Metropolitan Manila.

Jorge Yulo Architects & Associates

4F Karrivin Plaza, 2316 Chino Roces Extension, Makati City, Philippines

Tel: (632) 844-1502/26
Fax: (632) 844-2969
E-mail: jyaa@jorgeyulo.com

Joey Yupangco

Jose (Joey) Maria U. Yupangco studied industrial design at the Pratt Institute, Brooklyn (1984) and lighting design at the Parson's School of Design (1985). He obtained a Master's diploma from Domus Academy, Milan (1990), and did the graduate design program at the Architectural Association School of Architecture (1997–8). Based in New York in the 1980s, he worked on freelance projects and won early citations: Young Designer's Award (Pratt Institute, 1984), Finalist at the 2nd Osaka International Design Competition (1985), and 1st Place in the LIMN Furniture Design Competition, San Francisco (1986). He has been a Juror for the prestigious Japan-G Mark Design Asean Award for the last three years (2003–5). Since the 1990s, Yupangco has designed spaces for Manila's modernist restaurants, offices, and residences. Some of his published works are the Aguilar House, Soda Club, Chan House, La Gondola Restaurant, Neo Spa, Luna Penthouse of Rockwell, BCD Pinpoint, and TT8B Project. He runs Domani, a furniture showroom featuring Italian designs of tomorrow.

JY+A

Stores #9-10 New World Renaissance Hotel Arcade, Makati City, Philippines

Tel: (632) 811-6767
Fax: (632) 811-6707
E-mail: domain@ph.inter.net

Page 224 One side of the stunning V-shaped, mirror-image staircase in the Pedrosa courtyard house (page 98).

Acknowledgments

The author is grateful to the following people for their assistance during the production of this book:

Architect Emmanuel (Manny) Minaña, for design consultations on a quarter of the houses featured in the book, and also for his inspiration to bridge the intuitive and the literary and architectonic.

Josephine Knox and Carmen N. Pedrosa, for their hospitality and for access to their inspiring homes.

Dr and Mrs Victor Reyes for their hospitality in Tagaytay, Cavite.

Hans Juergen Sringer, for hospitality and accommodation for the photography team, and for being assistant to the assistant photographer.

SGS Designs Manila, who did the drawings.

Paulo Alcazaren for writing the Introduction and for co-ordinating the graphics.

And, especially, the home owners without whom this book would not have been possible:
Stephen and Marie Teresa Cheng
Beng and Rikki Dee
Toto and Lea Hilado
Josephine and Ervin Knox
Edwin and Alice Ngo
Argot Isidro and Manuel Sandejas
Nikki and Robbie Leviste
Regina Lopez
Arturo and Tessie Luz
Eduardo and Pilar Martinez-Miranda
Aurelio III and Gizela Montinola
Tes Pasola and Tony Gonzales
Aldonso and Carmen N. Pedrosa
Gunn and Cris Roque
Ricky and Veronica Sy
Al and Carla Tengco
Fernando and Catherine Zobel
Patsy Zobel and Alonso Halfttner
as well as those home owners who wish to remain anonymous.